GADAMER

IN CONVERSATION

Yale Studies in Hermeneutics

GADAMER
IN CONVERSATION

REFLECTIONS AND COMMENTARY

Hans-Georg Gadamer

With Carsten Dutt,

Glenn W. Most,

Alfons Grieder, and

Dörte von Westernhagen

Edited and

Translated by

Richard E. Palmer

YALE UNIVERSITY PRESS / NEW HAVEN & LONDON

Published with assistance from the Louis Stern Memorial Fund.

Designed by Mary Valencia.
Set in Janson Text type by The Composing Room of Michigan, Inc.,
Grand Rapids, Michigan.
Printed in the United States of America by Vail-Ballou Press,
Binghamton, New York.

Library of Congress Cataloging-in-Publication Data
Gadamer, Hans-Georg, 1900–
Gadamer in conversation : reflections and commentary / Hans-Georg Gadamer ; with
Carsten Dutt . . . [et al.] / edited and translated by Richard E. Palmer.
p.   cm. — (Yale studies in hermeneutics)
Includes bibliographical references and index.
ISBN 0-300-08488-9 (alk. paper)
1. Hermeneutics.   2. Aesthetics.   3. Practical philosophy.
I. Title.   II. Series.
2001004978

A catalogue record for this book is available from the British Library.

The paper in this book meets the guidelines for permanence and durability
of the Committee on Production Guidelines for Book Longevity
of the Council on Library Resources.

10 9 8 7 6 5 4 3 2 1

CONTENTS

v

PART II

PREFACE

Carsten Dutt's *Hermeneutik-Ästhetik-Praktische Philosophie: Gadamer im Gespräch* first came to my attention in Ziehank's, a Heidelberg bookstore facing the university square. The three topics in the title provoked my curiosity, since they are arguably the most important themes in Gadamer's thought. After buying and reading through it, I was struck by the engaging and intelligent way these topics were approached by Dutt in conversation with Gadamer and the accessibility that the philosophically heavy concepts of Gadamer acquired in the context of these conversations. It seemed to me, indeed, that these conversations could serve as an introduction to Gadamer for neophytes as well as a very interesting commentary for scholars familiar with the primary texts in question. This has been confirmed by the very favorable reviews and lively sales of the book in Germany, and its translation already into Italian, Japanese, Spanish and French. So I thought an English translation should also be welcome.

Checking with the German publisher, I made sure that it was not already being translated and then queried Yale University Press. They indicated an interest, so I submitted a draft translation for review. The publisher's reader was favorably impressed with the content and translation, but concerned that the book was really quite short. So, in consultation with Jean Grondin, I have selected three additional interviews for this volume. The first focuses on Gadamer's close association with the Greeks and classical philology. The second inquires into his relationship to phenomenology. The third is an inquiry into what it was like for philosophers in general and specifically Gadamer under the Nazis. Thus, the present volume supplements the delightful short book of Dutt's conversations with three other interviews on topics of interest to English-speaking readers.

Since Gadamer is known principally by his masterwork, *Truth and Method*, many English-speaking readers may not realize the extent to which his many other writings are now available in English. I have accordingly added a bibliographical appendix listing most books in English by and about Gadamer at the time of this translation. For reasons of space I did not include in this bibliography the nearly one hundred theses and dissertations on Gadamer nor the hundreds and hundreds of articles by and about Gadamer. I did, however, in the final section of the bibliographical appendices, give directions on how to locate theses and dissertations as well as articles by and on Gadamer in English.

INTRODUCTION

Hans-Georg Gadamer in conversation is vintage Gadamer. Genial, direct, and never at a loss, Gadamer in conversation is in his element. Throughout his career he liked nothing better than a good debate with a fellow philosopher, or a conversation with someone interested in his philosophy. Interviewers came from far and near, from universities and radio and television stations in Germany and all over the world. All were freely granted conversations. His famous debate in the late sixties with Jürgen Habermas, the internationally respected social philosopher, proved to be clarifying and productive for both parties.[1] His long-sought but all-too-brief encounter with Jacques Derrida at the Sorbonne in Paris in 1981 was not such a conversation; this was a great disappointment to him. A discussion of this encounter occurs in the second conversation.[2] It is important to note, also, that conversation as a topic figures importantly in Gadamer's hermeneutics and in his general philosophy.

The present volume will first offer a translation of the popular and much translated *Hermeneutik-Ästhetik-Praktische Philosophie: Gadamer im Gespräch* (already translated into Italian, Japanese, Spanish, and French, and forthcoming in Russian). The six conversations presented here should be of interest not only to persons who are just getting acquainted with Gadamer's thinking, but also to those who may already have read several of Gadamer's writings and would appreciate further light from the master himself about the major topics in his philosophy and life. The first two of the additional interviews were selected because phenomenology, the Greeks, and classical philology figure prominently in his thought, and these were not covered extensively in the first three conversations. The final interview was chosen because of a recent controversial book, published in German, about Gadamer during the Nazi period. In this final interview, conducted in 1989 by the daughter of a fallen SS officer and author of a book about children of Nazis, some probing questions are asked about how philosophers behaved under National Socialism and specifically how Gadamer himself as a non–National Socialist Party member was able to survive under a totalitarian dictatorship. Gadamer, as a mature adult during this period, was a precious living resource for the interviewer.

To help in the appreciation of this remarkable man who, born in 1900, experienced the beginning, middle, and end of the twentieth century, this introduction briefly sketches Gadamer's career as a philosopher, including his major works; discusses the special role of conversation in his philosophy itself; and summarizes each of the six conversations in this volume, introducing the partners in conversation and indicating a few of the topics covered.

Hans-Georg Gadamer

Born in Marburg, Germany, on February 11, 1900, Hans-Georg Gadamer has become one of the great wise men of twentieth-century philosophy.[3] He experienced the marvelous intellectual ferment at Marburg University in the 1920s, where he studied with the great classical philologist Paul Friedländer and knew such great classical philologists as Werner Jaeger, Eric Auerbach, and Julius Stenzel. While serving as assistant to Martin Heidegger at Marburg from 1923 to 1928, he wrote his advanced doctorate (*Habilitation*) under him,[4] completing it just as Heidegger was returning to Freiburg in 1928 to take the chair of Edmund Husserl. At Marburg during the 1920s and 1930s Gadamer would often go on Wednesday evenings to the home of dialectical theologian Rudolf Bultmann to study and discuss texts and theological matters with Bultmann and a close circle of his followers. Gadamer's friends and teachers from these years make up a roll-call of the movers and shakers in twentieth century thought.[5]

Yet life in Germany during the first half of this century, which included two world wars and the reign of Hitler, was also a distinct hardship for Gadamer, especially in terms of his career. The poor economy after the First World War meant that, after his *Habilitation* (certification of his second dissertation as qualifying him for a professor position) in 1928, there were few opportunities for the aspiring young professor of classical philosophy, so he remained a *Privatdozent* (unsalaried instructor) in the Department of Philosophy at Marburg. The rise of Hitler only made things worse, because the university system was politicized and preference in new appointments was given to members of the Nazi Party, which he refused to join. His teacher Paul Friedländer and a large number of his friends at Marburg were Jewish, so he witnessed firsthand the horror of Nazi racism. Despite his political beliefs, he did receive a couple of temporary positions, filling in for Jewish professors who had been fired.[6] A decade after his *Habilitation* he was called to Leipzig for a tenure-track position, and on January 1, 1939, he was named full professor and chair of the department—apparently in preference over two other candidates who were Nazis![7] In this rare case, not being a member of the Party worked in his favor (along with the recommendation of Count Gleispach). After the war his political quietism was rewarded by his election in 1945 as Rector in Leipzig because he was one of the few faculty members with virtually no involvement with the Nazis. His strategy at Leipzig during the repressive dictatorship of Hitler was to be as unobtrusive as possible. Gadamer remarked to me in a 1992 conversation that he and his liberal intellectual friends in Marburg had no use for Hitler's bigotry when he was beginning his climb to power, and they thought he surely could not last. But Hitler surprised them, and so Gadamer's cover during this difficult time was to present himself as a harmless specialist in classical Greek philosophy. As such, he posed no threat to anyone.[8]

The years after the Second World War also were hard times in Germany. When Gadamer received a call to assume a chair in Frankfurt in 1947, he was able to persuade the East German authorities that since he was born in Marburg he merely wanted to return to his home. This argument succeeded in part because of his friendship with some of the East German authorities with whom he had worked as Rector of Leipzig University. While in Frankfurt, he worked actively to restore Jewish professors, such as Theodor W. Adorno, to their former positions. Two years later, on January 1, 1949, he was invited to succeed Karl Jaspers as department head at the University of Heidelberg. He then actively set about to recall Jewish exiles, such as Karl Löwith, to occupy positions in the department, and he built Heidelberg into one of the most exciting centers for philosophy study in postwar Germany. His first years there were mainly concerned with building the department and meeting his teaching responsibilities, but during the 1950s he began offering lecture courses that became the basis for chapters in his masterwork, which was published in 1960.[9] Finally, at the age of sixty, after enduring Hitler and experiencing the hard times brought about by two world wars, he finally gave birth to his *magnum opus*.

Truth and Method instantly provoked lively discussion from both the left and right. The left claimed it offered an idealism of language that took no account of the material conditions that produce change. Habermas made this claim in his famous debate with Gadamer.[10] It was not political enough for the leftists; it did not even mention Marx while talking at length about Hegel. Furthermore, instead of starting from the Enlightenment assumption that the power of reason will enable us to make a totally new start, it actually defended prejudices as necessary for understanding anything. From the right, Emilio Betti, the historian of hermeneutics and author of a methodologically based version of hermeneutics, complained bitterly that Gadamer had trashed the great tradition of hermeneutics as a methodology for objectively determining textual meaning. In America, E. D. Hirsch, prompted by Betti, argued that Gadamer's emphasis on significance over textual meaning undermined the true mission of hermeneutics.[11] Gadamer's mentor, Heidegger, too, was disappointed. Gadamer, in an interview with me in 1992, noted that Heidegger reproached him for having deserted Heidegger's ontological leadership and for having been carried away by "phenomenological immanence." In addition, Heidegger said that Gadamer had never over-come the influence of his previous mentor, Paul Natorp. Gadamer's key term, *wirkungsgeschichtliches Bewußtsein* (consciousness in which history is at work), was, he said, just that—*consciousness*, a word Heidegger assid-uously avoided because of its associations with a metaphysics that needed to be outgrown. Gadamer's response to me was that he, too, was uncom-fortable with this word but could not find an alternative, so he had to use it for his argument about history in *Truth and Method*.

Yet the book's carefully developed arguments against both aesthetic consciousness and historical objectivity, its assertion of new concepts and terms, its formidable challenge to basic theoretical assumptions in the humanities and social sciences, and just the massive detail of its five hun-dred pages of argument, marked it as the most original and significant contribution to German philosophy since Heidegger's *Being and Time* (1927). Protestant theologians Gerhard Ebeling and Ernst Fuchs, fol-lowers of Bultmann and admirers of Heidegger, who were calling for a "new hermeneutic" in theology,[12] immediately hailed it as a turning point in twentieth century thought. In 1962, at Ebeling's "Institute for Hermeneutics" at Zurich, a whole course for theological students was dedicated to it. Special issues of philosophical journals were devoted to it in the 1960s. The young Jürgen Habermas came to Heidelberg to teach, calling for a new theory of knowledge in the social sciences. He joined dynamic and creative younger philosophy faculty like Ernst Tugendhat, Michael Theunissen, and Dieter Henrich. It was Gadamer's policy and style as chairman of the department to encourage debate and discussion, to foster and interpret not only Heideggerian thought but also the lega-cies of Aristotle, Descartes, Leibniz, Kant, Hegel, Kierkegaard, Husserl, and others. Professors from Oxford, like the Wittgenstein scholar An-thony Kenny, and American philosopher Stanley Cavell were among the visiting faculty during the two academic years I was there (1964–65, 1971–72). Gadamer came to be recognized as one of the foremost in-terpreters of Heidegger's thought in Germany, although Wilhelm von Herrmann in Freiburg was certainly more rigorously faithful to the exact interpretation of the master, and Otto Pöggeler at Bochum was interna-tionally respected. In America, Father Richardson's book on Heidegger fanned the interest of English-speaking readers in Heidegger's thought, and opened the path for his follower Gadamer when he came to the United States, and societies dedicated to the study of Heidegger, Husserl, and phenomenology were founded during the 1960s.[13]

After the publication of *Truth and Method* in 1960, reviews, articles, and even short books of favorable and unfavorable comment poured in, and Gadamer set about answering his critics as he continued to give lecture courses and offer seminars. To the second edition in 1965, and third edition of 1971, he appended lengthy replies and clarifications. It is fair to say that Gadamer spent a good part of his time during the forty years since 1960 explaining and defending *Truth and Method*—sometimes also admitting its shortcomings, especially the deficiencies of the third part, which he had not had time to develop fully. In 1960, few could foresee that another four decades of scholarly work and a dozen other important books or collections of essays on various topics would follow the appearance of that masterwork, and that even in his nineties Gadamer would be publishing more books and conducting the interpretive conversations collected in this volume.

Fame came late, but it came with great fullness, and after his retirement in 1968, Gadamer was invited to lecture all over Europe and in Africa, Japan, and North and South America. Virtually every year he spent a semester or more at a university in the United States or Canada, including Vanderbilt, University of Dallas, Catholic University of America (Washington, D.C.), McMasters University in Hamilton, Ontario, Canada (where he also received an honorary doctorate), and repeatedly at Boston College even into the 1980s. During these years, the universities at which he was in residence served as bases from which to accept invitations to lecture all over America: Syracuse University, University of Wisconsin at Milwaukee, Northwestern University, annual meetings of the Society for Phenomenology and Existential Philosophy and the American Academy of Religion, to name but a few.[14] In 1976, the translation into English of both *Truth and Method* and *Philosophical Hermeneutics*, which is a collection of his essays, suddenly made Gadamer's own writings accessible to English-speakers, and his friendliness, openness to questions, and determination to lecture in English despite little experience in speaking that language (his Italian and French were far more fluent) all made him a highly desirable guest lecturer. Many American (and other) graduate students were eager to translate his writings, and these began to appear in scholarly journals. Many of his visiting lectures were taped, edited, and published. Collections of his writings on Plato, Hegel, and Heidegger, along with *The Relevance of the Beautiful* (1986) and *Reason in an Age of Science* (1981), to name a few, started to appear in English beginning in 1976 with *Hegel's Dialectic* (Yale) and continuing in the 1980s and 1990s.[15] His books of essays on poetry and literary theory, such as *Poetica* (1977) and its enlarged second edition titled *Gedicht und Gespräch* (1990), were not translated, but many of the essays in them appeared in *The Relevance of the Beautiful and Other Essays* (1986), *Hans-Georg Gadamer on Education, Poetry, and History: Applied Hermeneutics* (1992), and *Literature and Philosophy in Dialogue: Essays in German Literary Theory* (1994).

The relevance of philosophical hermeneutics to other disciplines began to be perceived more and more widely, first in Germany and then in many other parts of the world.[16] As of 2000, *Truth and Method* had been translated (all or in part) into thirteen languages.[17] The monumental bibliography of just Gadamer's own writings, 348 pages in length, by Etsuro Makita, routinely lists a half-dozen languages into which a given essay has been translated.[18] Many honors came. Gadamer was invited into honorary membership in learned scholarly societies in Italy, Greece, Hungary, Canada, America, and Germany, and he was awarded eight honorary doctorates.[19] Criticisms raised from the left by Jürgen Habermas in the late 1960s and early 1970s only added fuel to the fire.

The encounter with Jacques Derrida that Gadamer had eagerly anticipated took place in Paris in 1981. With Derrida's growing popularity in the United States a rivalry developed between the followers of French deconstruction and the followers of German hermeneutics. Although Derrida later referred to the encounter as a nonevent, it did help to draw the lines more clearly between Gadamer's hermeneutical and Derrida's deconstructionist thought.[20] In an effort at documenting a French alternative to the tradition of philosophical hermeneutics and placing the Derridian deconstructive hermeneutics in context, Gayle Ormiston and Alan Schrift published as companion volumes in 1990 *The Hermeneutic Tradition: From Ast to Ricoeur* and *Transforming the Hermeneutic Context: The French Connection*.[21] On behalf of a Derridian standpoint, John D.

Caputo directly attacked Gadamer in his *Radical Hermeneutics*, labeling Gadamer a "closet essentialist" committed to "eternal truths."[22] This accusation glosses over the fact that Gadamer's philosophical hermeneutics and Derrida's deconstruction are both forms of hermeneutics growing out of Heidegger's hermeneutic of facticity. In an article on these two contrasting thinkers I concluded that they were two quite different and important thinkers; their positions do not cancel each other out but rather valuably "supplement" one another.[23]

Gadamer's final major project, which occupied him from 1984 to 1995, was to gather together, reread, correct, and in some cases significantly revise his writings into a collected edition—the *Gesammelte Werke* (Tübingen: Mohr, 1985–1995). The result was ten volumes, each averaging about 450 pages and containing about forty essays or chapters of books. In other words, the ten volumes of the *Gesammelte Werke (GW)* offer well over 300 articles and essays. Gadamer chose not to include many of his writings, such as his essays originally published in English, Italian, or French, unless they had been translated back into German. The *GW,* however, does contain *Truth and Method* as its first volume, and in the other volumes are most of the scholarly essays that make up his book-length collections of essays on different topics. But virtually none of his hundreds of book reviews was included. He also omitted most of the occasional nonphilosophical pieces that he wrote over the years, such as introductions for a musical festival, an art exhibition, or for a book collecting the paintings of an artist, as he did for his deceased son-in-law.[24] Nor did he include any of his many interviews and panel discussions for radio, television, or newspapers.[25] In other words, the ten volumes of the *Gesammelte Werke* represent a selection of works Gadamer considered to be of long-term interest. They are not an inclusive collection of Gadamer's very extensive writings.

In a number of cases Gadamer also included previously unpublished essays in the *Gesammelte Werke*; for instance, the two important 1992 essays on art and language that conclude Volume 8. Also not included were several books by Gadamer that were not published until the 1990s, even in German, such as a collection of Gadamer's essays on the topic of health, *Die Unverborgenheit der Gesundheit* (1993), which soon appeared in English as *The Enigma of Health* (1995).[26] Only three essays from that book appear in *GW.* Gadamer also surprised his followers with two other books which first appeared in the late 1990s: *Der Anfang der Philosophie* (1996), a series of 1989 lectures that he gave in Italian on Presocratic philosophy, focusing on Parmenides, and that were published in that language (subsequently translated back into German and immediately into English by Rod Coltman as *The Beginning of Philosophy* [1998]); and *Der Anfang des Wissens*, a parallel volume of balancing (earlier) essays on Heraclitus and early Greek Presocratic philosophy, which appeared in 1999 and will be published as *The Beginning of Knowledge*, translated by Rod Coltman, in late 2001. Finally, in 2000, Mohr Siebeck published a diverse collection of essays titled *Hermeneutische Entwürfe* (*Hermeneutical Projects*) that were not included in the collected works, effectively amounting to a 250-page (shorter) eleventh volume of the collected works.

Turning to the *Gesammelte Werke*, one is surprised by the range of Gadamer's writings within its ten volumes. Only volumes 1, 2, and 10 contain essays generally focused on the topic of hermeneutics. Volumes 3 and 4 collect his writings on modern philosophy, especially Hegel, Husserl, and Heidegger. Volumes 5 through 7 contain essays on Greek philosophy. Volume 8 deals with theory and philosophy of art in general, and Volume 9 offers interpretations of specific authors and works of literature. Volume 10 includes seven essays on Heidegger written since *Heidegger's Ways* (1983), fifteen essays on hermeneutics written since Volume 2 appeared in 1986, ten essays commenting on the place of philosophy in society, and thirteen remembrances of major figures in Germany whom Gadamer had had the good fortune to know. At the end of Volume 10 are tables of contents of all ten volumes of *GW,* and, among other indexes, there is a list of 110 of Gadamer's essays in English (pp. 472–476).

Gadamer was not afraid to write about science, politics, health, music, poetry, philosophy, theology, or his recollections of famous people. He became the grand old man of philosophy and accepted innumerable invitations to speak. His personal recollections of Heidegger and his insightful interpretations of Heideggerian texts were among his favorite topics and were eagerly received. He gathered these into the 1983 book *Heideggers Wege* (translated in 1994 as *Heidegger's Ways*), and seven subsequent essays on Heidegger were gathered into a section in *GW* 10. Interviews with Gadamer have been published in many languages because he graciously consented to interview requests from all over the world. Interviews could be done in Italian, French, or English, as Gadamer spoke these languages fluently. These interviews themselves form a distinct genre in which Gadamer gives free expression to his ideas, a less formal and more accessible medium that always takes into account the background of the interviewer. Interviews offer us a valuable medium of expression for Gadamer's ideas, a medium that stands outside his collected works yet comments on them. Interviews also show the personal side of Gadamer to great advantage because he was a master of conversation: always open, tolerant, and amazingly quick in his recall of an infinite number of topics. The six conversations in *Gadamer in Conversation*, all published in the 1990s, give the reader a good sample of this genre.[27]

Conversation

In the first conversation here, Gadamer says that conversation itself "is the essence of what I have been working on over the past thirty years." Why does conversation occupy such a special place in Gadamer's philosophy and in his life? Philosophically, there are several reasons. First, his earliest serious philosophical study was of Plato and Socrates, masters of dialogue. For Socrates as for Gadamer, dialogue was not just a means of passing the time in pleasant but aimless conversation; it was an intense, restless, and unending quest for truth. Such a quest would have no meaning if one assumed oneself to have a hammerlock on the truth; rather, one has to assume that one's interlocutor could be right, or at least could show you something you did not know. Thus, like Socrates, Gadamer would even try to strengthen the other person's argument, trying to see the matter from the other point of view. Gadamer was always ready to learn something from the other person in a conversation, always more loyal to the truth than to his own view of it. He assumed with Hegel that "die Wahrheit ist das Ganze" (the truth is the whole), so every specific view of truth is necessarily partial, fallible, and correctable in the light of new knowledge. His reply to many arguments began with, "Ich gebe zu, daß"—(I concede that ...). The interlocutor was always granted respect. Like Plato and Hegel, Gadamer is profoundly dialectical in his style of thinking.

Second, because the encounter with another person, especially someone from another region or country, involved for Gadamer something like an encounter with another horizon, and he tried hard to appreciate the otherness of the other's horizon of understanding. He almost always seemed to be able to find common ground. For Gadamer, the otherness of the other person's horizon serves to enrich one's own horizon. It is not a threat.

Third, in a larger sense, hermeneutics in practice is itself a conversation, even when it is a conversation with a text. One gains most when one learns something new from the text, when one has to change one's opinion, when the speaking of the text restructures one's self-understanding.[28] This partially explains why Gadamer encouraged his followers at Heidelberg to be critical and to go their own way, to find other philosophers to interpret rather than become dogmatic exponents of philosophical hermeneutics. He had more respect for someone who disagreed with him and was willing to argue for that position than for someone who followed him with dogmatic loyalty. In fact, following the Platonic principle of *eumenes elenchoi*—which means that the interlocutor could be right—he eagerly explored counterarguments in quest of the truth. Such was his unflagging faith in reason. His first response to challenges was to find wherein both parties agreed, to concede a part of the argument, and then, like Socrates, find "just one small point" on which he wanted to know more, or where he wondered if the presuppositions were tenable.

When one is in conversation with a text, the text also speaks, just as another person speaks. Likewise, Gadamer emphasizes that it is *within a linguistic horizon* that an encounter with artwork or text takes place. In the conversations in this book, especially in the second conversation, which takes up deconstruction and its emphasis on writtenness, Gadamer repeatedly emphasizes the primacy of "living language," language that speaks and in its speaking brings about events of disclosure. Even the written word that one construes, according to Gadamer, must be brought to life, must be enabled to speak.

"Understanding," a key word in Gadamer's hermeneutics, is, in the deeper sense, an event of the disclosure of truth, an event which in true conversation is reached by the partners together. But it is important to avoid Platonic metaphysics in cognizing the disclosure of truth. For

Gadamer, following Heidegger, this is not a disclosure of some eternal, changeless essence; rather, for Gadamer it yields an existential sense that "this is the way things are." In the presence of great art, says Gadamer, one says to oneself, "So ist es!" (Yes, that's how things are!) The truth may be painful, disappointing, even tragic; it may shatter one's whole previous view of life, but ultimately one says, according to Gadamer, "So ist es!" Beethoven in one of his very late sonatas or quartets writes in the score: "Ist es so?" and the answer comes, "Es ist so." The ontological word "is" is deeply implicated with truth. It is not an essentialist but an existential truth; it is not an infinite but a finite, fallible truth, emerging in an experiential, lived encounter. This is part of the legacy of Heidegger, who also sees truth as an event, as something that happens. For both Gadamer and Heidegger, to encounter a piece of artwork is to experience truth emerging, truth happening, truth *being*. Gadamer holds that language comes into its own in living speech but comes most truly into its own in poetic texts, which we resurrect inwardly into the intonations of spoken language as we read them. He follows Heidegger in this view, but unlike his distinguished teacher, who published a small book of poems,[29] Gadamer has spared us any poetry of his own. Still, the reading of great poetry remains a necessary part of his own daily life, and he devotes many essays to its interpretation.[30] He says it keeps him in contact with what is most vital and true in life. For instance, he told me that he prepared for his trip to America by reading the poetry of Wallace Stephens. But to communicate with others, Gadamer chooses living conversation, not poetry.

It should be remembered that Friedrich Schleiermacher, the father of modern philosophical hermeneutics, was known to be a master at conversation. Conversation, for Schleiermacher, was a model for the event of understanding. In a conversation there is another person, there are words exchanged, and there is the act of construing the words. Understanding, for Schleiermacher, is, in its essence, like understanding another person in conversation; in conversation one senses the style, one guesses the meaning of a thou.[31] But for Gadamer in *Truth and Method*, it is not the "dark thou," the soul of the other, that is to be penetrated psychologically; rather it is the "matter" (the *Sache*) that the words in their richness reveal; it is the assertion by the words that *speaks* and is heard in its meaning. For Gadamer, the process of understanding a printed text causes language to become living language, a speaking that urgently conveys a "matter" (*Sache*) to be understood. Drawing back from the psychological element in Schleiermacher, Gadamer proposes to follow Hegel and Plato more than Schleiermacher in his view of conversation, emphasizing the dialectical interplay of ideas rather than an empathetic sensing of feelings that leads to a perception of the very soul of the other.

Gadamer's strong thematic emphasis on conversation contrasts with both Heidegger and Derrida. In his essay "*Destruktion* and Deconstruction," Gadamer asserts that "to be in a conversation means to be beyond oneself, to think with the other and to come back to oneself as if to another."[32] Granted, Heidegger agrees with Hölderlin that "we are a conversation," but Heidegger's conversation seems to be that of the thinker on a solitary walk through the forest paths of thought. Its goal is to bring others to his vision, to show us how we moderns have been misled by a covertly present metaphysics of substance. Derrida, like Heidegger, is not a liberal, Socratic inquirer, always asserting on principle that the other person really could be right.[33] His passion, following Heidegger, is to unmask the logocentrism of Western metaphysics, to unmask the naive metaphysical assumptions of linguistics theory, a theory that goes back to an oral rather than a written word. For Derrida, it is the structure of apprehending the written word that is able to show us the moment of absence in language, a moment that is lost in Saussure's linguistics with its theoretical primacy of oral speech.[34] Thus, Derrida claims that he is the true inheritor of Heidegger's destruction of Western metaphysics, of the "metaphysics of presence."

Gadamer bitterly complained to me in 1992 that "Derrida is not capable of dialogue, only monologue." But there were definable reasons why Derrida resisted dialogue with Gadamer. Commenting on their 1981 encounter,[35] Josef Simon pointed out that Derrida did not want to be co-opted; he was resisting Gadamer's assumption that their respect for, and debt to, Heidegger would afford them common ground, and that they would therefore have much to debate regarding the interpretation of Heidegger.[36] From Gadamer's point of view, as champions of the Heideggerian legacy, he and Derrida were already in the same camp. For Derrida, however, Gadamer had betrayed that legacy.

In his 1981 encounter with Derrida in Paris, Gadamer presented a paper that dealt extensively with Derrida's philosophy, but Derrida's paper, "Interpreting Signatures (Heidegger/Nietzsche)," did not even mention Gadamer; instead he undertook a critique of Heidegger's unifying tendency in boiling Nietzsche's thought down to two principles.[37] Against this view, Derrida portrayed Nietzsche as a man who wears many masks. Clearly Derrida wanted no rapprochement with Gadamer today, thank you! A subsequent sharing of the speaker's stand with Gadamer in Heidelberg in 1989 on the topic of Heidegger's politics again brought no productive dialogue between Derrida and Gadamer, according to Gadamer, even though Gadamer was speaking in French. Dialogue with Gadamer seems to be a risk Derrida avoided, in part because this would entail reading Gadamer's writings in German, and Derrida freely admitted later that he had not had time to do so for their 1981 encounter.[38] But by frustrating Gadamer's efforts at dialogue, Derrida was implicitly denying the claim of philosophical hermeneutics to universality. Gadamer's reply was that Derrida, like everyone else, wishes to communicate or he would not be speaking and writing.[39] In this case, we seem to come up against the limits of conversation and Gadamer's concept of it.

We could also note that, just as in the dialogues of Plato, in the six conversations in this volume the master seems to end up doing most of the talking. Gadamer is the great philosopher explaining what he was doing and what he was not doing. But this is a special value of the conversations. They are not ordinary conversations but rather discussions among experts with the master in his nineties. Dutt, Most, and Grieder are all well acquainted with Gadamer's writings. Dörte von Westernhagen, however, comes as an inquirer into Gadamer's complicity with the Nazis. She is an expert on the period but not on Gadamer's philosophy. These conversations, then, taken together represent Gadamer's final clarifications and defense of his evolving position, how it developed, and its relation to such topics as Aristotle, Plato, Heidegger, Husserl, Derrida, hermeneutics, art, history, classical philology, the Greeks, phenomenology, and his relationship with the Nazis. The conversations are not framed in the highly technical prose of most monological essays in philosophy but in the mode of active conversation. For this reason, I believe that the conversations presented here may make Gadamer's philosophical views more lively and accessible than do the monological prose in which some of his interpreters try to explain them.

In conclusion, Gadamer is a formidable partner in philosophical debate, but to read Gadamer in conversation is not just to allow him the medium best suited for his own personal talent, style, and preference. Conversation, as we have seen, is itself also a central issue and theme in his philosophical hermeneutics. Gadamer explains many dimensions of hermeneutics by drawing on the nature of dialogue in Plato and of dialectic in Hegel. Deeply involved is Gadamer's view of language in relation to hermeneutics. Gadamer resolutely insists on the role of "living language" in understanding, even in the understanding of written texts. To be understood, language must live, and it is truly alive in these conversations.

The Six Conversations

Given the central importance of conversation in Gadamer's philosophy, it was a fortunate event when, in 1993, Gadamer consented to engage in a series of reflective conversations on his philosophy with Carsten Dutt, a brilliant young *Assistent* in the Philosophy Seminar at the University of Heidelberg. Dutt had previously studied at the University of Konstanz and had a strong background in both literature and philosophy. The interviews were published in the same year under the title, *Hermeneutik-Ästhetik-Praktische Philosophie: Gadamer im Gespräch* (Hermeneutics, Aesthetics, Practical Philosophy: Gadamer in Conversation); they form the first half of the present volume and give it its title. The conversations with Dutt, framed for publication as three lengthy interviews with Gadamer at his home in Ziegelhausen, a small town adjoining Heidelberg, were published by a local publisher as a slender, eighty-page volume.[40] Friendly and informal, they focus on what are probably the three most important themes of Gadamer's philosophical output: hermeneutics, aesthetics, and practical philosophy.

The first conversation is about hermeneutics and focuses primarily on *Truth and Method*. The interview takes up three major concepts in the masterwork that have provoked angry critical objections since its publication.[41] Gadamer explains these three concepts and replies to the major critics of his position here much more briefly than he had done in the lengthy supplements to the second and third editions of the master-work.[42] In this first conversation, he begins by pointing out that *Truth and Method* is not intended to be a methodology for the human sciences but a philosophy of interpretation. He notes that it must have surprised his readers who expected the steps of a method of interpretation, that instead he turns to the experience of art as the key to his hermeneutical philosophy. Language, history, and his relation to Heidegger are other topics in this, the longest of the three conversations with Dutt.

Aesthetics is the general theme of the second conversation. Dutt wastes no time in going back to the failed encounter with Derrida and Gadamer's relation to deconstruction. Gadamer says that the difference between himself and Derrida is that Derrida does not want to reach an understanding and even may have an "incapacity for dialogue." With regard to the attempt in literary theory to apply his philosophical hermeneutics, Dutt takes up Hans-Robert Jauss's and Rainer Warning's attempts to develop an aesthetics of reception based on *Truth and Method*. In doing so, Gadamer says, Jauss and Warning did not understand him, especially in relation to the example of the classical, which they criticize. Gadamer also discusses his key concept of the "eminent text," a text which derives its power from itself and not from its author. He explains his important concept of *Gleichzeitigkeit* (simultaneity), the power of artworks of the past to be present and meaningful here and now: "One does not have the meaning of a work of art in such a way that one can speak of a transfer of meaning. A work of art *must be there itself.* For carriers of meaning you can find substitutes." He points to a painting in his study by Serge Poliakoff (1906–1969), presented to him thirty years earlier by his students. Although he cannot put into words what the painting says, it still compels him to come back to it again at again.

The third conversation takes up *practical philosophy* and with it the question of ethics. Practical philosophy, especially exemplified in the Greek term *phronesis* (practical wisdom), looms large in Gadamer's thought, and he goes back to this Greek term that does not seek the exactness of numbers but the more intuitive wisdom of measure and moderation. "*Phronesis*," he says, "proves itself only in the concrete situation and always already stands within a living network of common convictions, habits, and values—that is to say, an *ethos.*" Thus, human reasoning about ethics must go back to the solidarities that hold human beings together. In this respect Gadamer essentially agrees with Aristotle that man is a political animal. At one point Dutt asks, "So must we not try above all to advance the public discussion?" and Gadamer answers, "Yes, but one must do more than advance the public discussion. One must also do something oneself!" Philosophy is not just theory, it is practical, embedded in the matrix of everyday human activity, a matrix requiring decisions and action. Because Gadamer looks for "the resources of social reason," his thought has been also of interest to social thinkers and not just to humanists. His thought, as he notes here, is neither idealistically utopian on the one hand, nor pessimistic and nihilistic on the other. His faith in reason is faith in a socially embedded, situational, linguistic, practical reason and reasoning.

To the three interviews with Carsten Dutt we have added three other conversations which take up dimensions of Gadamer's thought not covered in Dutt's conversations but which may be of interest to English-speaking readers: the Greeks, phenomenology, and how he managed to survive under National Socialism.

The first of the additional conversations, titled "The Greeks, Our Teachers," takes up the seminal role that the Greeks play in Gadamer's thought. Conducting the interview is Glenn W. Most, a professor of classical philology at the University of Heidelberg and a long-time friend of Professor Gadamer. The interview begins with Gadamer recalling the negative impression that his gymnasium instruction in Greek made on him in Breslau, which caused him to focus his university studies on literature and philosophy rather than on classical philology, although this was a strong subject area at Marburg. He tells of first turning to the philosopher Paul Natorp, then to Nikolai Hartmann, and then to Martin Heidegger. He explains his later decision to immerse himself in classical philology at Marburg as an effort to gain a counterbalance to the powerful spell of Heidegger's interpretive skill. Other subjects discussed in this conversation are: our access to Presocratic philosophy, Plato and democracy, the anticipation of *phronesis* in Plato, the contrast between Greek and modern philosophers, common ground with analytic philosophy, and finally the "immediate conceptual power" of Greek as a spoken language." This leads to the question of the relevance of Greek thought to the present situation of philosophy within our culture.

The next conversation, dating from 1992, was on phenomenology and Gadamer's place in the phenomenological tradition.[43] The interviewer, Alfons Grieder, titled it simply "A Conversation with Hans-Georg Gadamer" and translated it into English for the May 1995 issue of the *Journal of the British Society for Phenomenology* (vol. 26, no.2: 16–26). We have retitled it "On Phenomenology," since that is its manifest topic. Although this conversation is already available in English in that distinguished journal (the other five conversations appear here for the first time in English), the interview adds a special dimension to the set of conversations offered here: It adds not only Gadamer's unique recollections and experience of phenomenology but also explores the extent to which Gadamer sees his own work as an extension of phenomenology. Gadamer was situated at a key point historically in relation to phenomenology. Born in 1900, he was in his twenties during the exciting heyday of the philosophy of Husserl and Heidegger's championing of it at Marburg. So the discussion has historical and biographical interest as well as philosophical. The conversation takes up Gadamer's first encounter with phenomenology while at Marburg, his own interactions with the philosophy of Husserl at Freiburg and Marburg, and then his experience of Heidegger's ambiguous championing of phenomenology at Marburg. It also goes into Gadamer's relationship to life-philosopher Georg Misch, Wilhelm Dilthey's son-in-law and follower, and the philosophy of Dilthey as Gadamer discussed it in *Truth and Method*. The last part of the interview probes his own claim to being a phenomenologist and contrasts it with that of Martin Heidegger. What Gadamer says is that, yes, he is a phenomenologist, but one who, like Heidegger and Scheler, has tried to mobilize the resources of phenomenology in a creative way. Some inheritors of the phenomenological tradition turn it into a form of scholasticism, but he regards his inheritance of phenomenology as more creative and productive than this. His philosophical hermeneutics is also a phenomenological hermeneutics. It is interesting to note that Professor Dermot Moran's recent *Introduction to Phenomenology* sees "an essential connection between phenomenology and hermeneutics" and devotes a thirty-eight-page chapter to Gadamer's thought.[44]

The final interview differs from the others in several ways. First, it is not about Gadamer's philosophy but about his life during the Nazi period. This interview occurred in 1989, nearly forty-five years after the fall of Nazi Germany, so fewer and fewer persons were still living who had firsthand recollections of National Socialism. The interview therefore was very much an information-gathering session to record Gadamer's recollections. A major objective of the interview was to gauge the degree of cooperation and complicity of philosophy professors under fascist dictatorship. What accommodations did Gadamer remember his fellow philosophers making under Hitler? Did some or many of them actively promote National Socialism in their lectures in order to please the authorities? In what ways did Gadamer himself have to cooperate with National Socialism in order to survive under Hitler?

Second, there was a contrast with the interlocutors in the other conversations. Unlike the previous friendly interviewers, who were well versed in his writings and were trying to draw Gadamer out on different areas of his contributions to philosophy, Dörte von Westernhagen was most interested his collaboration with the Nazis and that of other colleagues under Hitler. She was not concerned with Gadamer's philosophy and did not ask a single question about it. Born in 1943, the daughter of a fallen SS officer, she was well acquainted with the period through extensive research for her book *Die Kinder der Täter: das Dritte Reich und die Generation danach* (*Children of the [Evil-] Doers: The Third Reich and the Generation After*).[45] Her questions show that she had already made efforts to inquire into the activities of professors, for in many cases her questions to Gadamer sought confirmation of her previous research.

Third, this interview gets into political dimensions and personal ethical choices not covered in the previous interviews. Information on this topic has a special relevance in light of a German doctoral dissertation on Gadamer and the Nazis by Teresa Orozco, which attempted a more in-depth investigation into Gadamer's presumed complicity with the Nazis. This dissertation, *Platonische Gewalt: Gadamers Politische Hermeneutik der NS-Zeit* (*Platonic Violence: Gadamer's Political Hermeneutics of the National Socialist Era*) was published by Argument Verlag, the same press that earlier published the present interview.[46] It was part of a general research program investigating what happened in German philosophy under Hitler. Shortly after the Orozco book appeared, I asked Professor Gadamer whether he intended to reply to the many unfair charges and innuendoes that it contains, and he said no. Why? Because it would dignify the book with an attention it did not deserve, he said. Also, he noted that he had already freely discussed this period of his life on many occasions, which were part of the public record. The interview published here was one of those occasions. It constitutes a valuable reply (before the fact) to the allegations in Orozco's book.

The title of Orozco's 1995 book, *Platonic Violence*, proclaims Gadamer's alleged guilt of violence, albeit of a Platonic kind, and the subtitle *Gadamer's Political Hermeneutics of the National Socialist Era* asserts that he offered a political hermeneutics during the Nazi era. Both accusations are false. The series title, too, "Ideological Powers of National Socialism," wrongly implies that Gadamer was an active source of Nazi ideology, another absurd libel. Orozco's principal historical/biographical evidence is that Gadamer signed a 1933 document of support for Hitler directed to foreign countries and that during the Nazi period he participated in a Nazi orientation camp and published two articles on Plato and one on Herder. The fact that Gadamer was a specialist in Plato long before the Hitler era, having written a doctoral dissertation on Plato in 1922 and his habilitation in 1929 on *Plato's Dialectical Ethics*, which was published in 1931, was treated as irrelevant. The further writings on Plato were obviously done solely to please the Nazis, according to Orozco, although this was not the case at all. We see this quite clearly in Gadamer's "Selbstdarstellung," now translated as part of his "Reflections on a Philosophical Journey" (pp. 3–18, 26–40), which discusses the writings and life during the war and the occasions that gave rise to these reflections.[47] It is the best personal account by Gadamer available in English.[48] He mentions, in one case, that in giving a talk to French prisoners of war (in French, of course), he gave a classical quote, "An empire that extends itself beyond measure, beyond moderation is *auprès de sa chute*—near its fall."[49] The French officers looked at each other meaningfully and got the message, while the Nazi overseers present only laughed at the clever remark. Regarding his 1934 publication on Plato and the poets he remarks that Plato's utopia "has more to do with Jonathan Swift than political science. My publication of this essay in 1934 documents my position vis-à-vis National Socialism with the motto placed at the beginning: *Whoever philosophizes will not be in agreement with the times.*"⁵⁰ Again, the motto was too subtle for the Nazis to notice. In any case, two publications on Plato and one on Herder—none of which make any reference whatsoever to National Socialism—did not make Gadamer an "ideological power" of National Socialism, nor do the rest of the facts taken out of context and the innuendos in the Orozco book make Gadamer an architect of National Socialist ideology.

Fortunately, Jean Grondin's definitive *Hans-Georg Gadamer: Eine Biographie*, published in 1999,⁵¹ sets the record straight, and a translation is to be published by Yale University Press. It devotes three chapters to Gadamer's life during this period and paints a well-documented picture of Gadamer's liberal political views, which he had to stifle, and his clear abstention from politics during that period. While Heidegger's connections with the Nazis are well documented, Gadamer's are minimal: signing a statement of support of Hitler in 1933 when failure to do so would have led to his expulsion from Germany; attending an orientation camp for teachers in October 1935 with the hope of getting a job in philosophy; and giving a talk on "Folk [meaning *Volk*, a people, as in the German people] and History in Herder's Thought" in France in May 1941 at the invitation of a long-time professional friend from Marburg. His invitation to occupy a chair at Leipzig a couple of years after the camp was, in fact, with the recommendation of the director of the camp he attended. In all of these cases, we see that Gadamer, a nonmember of the Party with only scorn for its policies, a man whose closest friends were Jewish, was not an "ideological power" working in support of National Socialism, but rather a professor of ancient philosophy surviving and getting on with his life under the terror of a fascist police state. In Leipzig he became a popular lecturer with the students and chair of the department, but he said nothing from the lectern in support of the Nazis. In fact, because he was department chair, he was able to decline invitations to collaborate on Nazi projects with the excuse that his many duties did not leave him time. He notes that several times during his Leipzig period he was denounced by Nazis or Nazi sympathizers, but the rector, a close friend and colleague, would on each occasion call him in and then formally dismiss the charges.

We see from the interview with von Westernhagen, and in much greater detail in Grondin's biography, that Gadamer was far from an "ideological power" in National Socialism. He never at any time considered joining the Nazi Party. Until 1933 he and his circle of liberal intellectual friends at Marburg regarded Hitler and the Nazi Party as too stupid ever to be accepted by the electorate. His closest colleagues and dear teachers in Marburg were Jewish, and he did all he could to protect them and corresponded with them after they emigrated from Germany. He detested Hitler's racist policy. Politically, he hoped Hitler would last only a short time and be gone. In 1938, with the declaration of war, he and many others suddenly realized that Hitler was a madman and a catastrophe for the country.

Many Germans were depressed, fearful, and desperate after 1938. Several assassination attempts on Hitler were thwarted and all those in complicity executed. Gadamer's strategy in this period was to retreat behind the protective walls of his special discipline, ancient Greek philosophy, to cooperate as little as possible with the Nazis while doing as much as he could for his Jewish friends, and through cleverness to survive the nightmare. As he says at the end of the interview, his dual goal was to survive and to keep the confidence of his Jewish friends. After the nightmare was over and the war ended, he was made rector of the University of Leipzig principally because he was very popular in the university and had absolutely no ties with the Nazis. True, he had Nazi colleagues even in his own department, but he treated them with respect for their professional work and resolutely avoided all discussion of politics. Indeed, as Grondin makes clear, Gadamer was hired in 1938 in preference to two other candidates with better political credentials and publication records largely because the department did *not* want to hire a committed member of the Party. Leipzig was one of the universities that, during the war, the Nazis did not attempt to dominate ideologically. Of course professors and students could not publicly criticize or attack the Nazis, and the perception was that the Gestapo was everywhere so everyone had to be careful, but Nazis did not intrude on the departmental selection decisions as they had at Kiel. In fact, the title of the interview derives from Gadamer's remark that in Leipzig (and elsewhere) the "real Nazis" did not see university professors as a major threat. He said: "The real Nazis had no interest at all in us." Unless the professor was either Jewish, politically active against National Socialism, or plotting against Hitler, at Leipzig University he or she was left alone. One had to be discreet, of course. Gadamer's student assistant at the time, Käte Lekebusch, was unwise enough to remark casually to a friend after a failed assassination attempt that she would be delighted if someone would shoot Hitler. She was arrested, nearly raped, and incarcerated; she would have been tried and executed, but invading Russian troops arrived just in time. Five years later she and Gadamer were married. This was his second marriage.

We are now in a position to put some of the questions and answers in the interview with von Westernhagen in context. The first question was: "In 1933 what professors had to go?" It interested me that there were no pleasantries, no expressions of thanks for the opportunity to have the interview, or special gestures of respect for a philosopher of his stature. Perhaps these were present but not included in the published text. The tone seems almost inquisitorial. But Gadamer ignores this and points out that the process did not take place all at once, that it was much more gradual in academic circles than in the government. Next, she asked about Richard Kroner, the Jewish professor whose place Gadamer took at Kiel in 1934–35. They were special friends and Gadamer recalls their sad encounter when he arrived in Kiel. Kroner in no way blamed Gadamer for what the Nazis did to him, and Gadamer, desperate for a job, accepted the offer. He had a wife and daughter to support. She asks about Kurt Hildebrandt, an idealistic conservative, a follower of the poet Stefan George, and Gadamer suggests that his friendship with him, a member of the George circle, may have figured in his being hired. Again, Hitler's promise to rebuild Germany, but not necessarily his racism, appealed to patriotic conservatives.

Her question about "right-wing conservatives who took advantage of the moment in 1933" draws a reproach from Gadamer: "You express it in a perhaps too unfriendly way. . . . I don't think one should malign these people." Like most patriotic Germans, they were misled. Even in the discussion of Erich Rothacker, whose opportunism and methods he hated, Gadamer concedes that he was "no dumbbell" and that "he was a tremendously wide reader and excellent moderator" and also that he commanded the loyalty of students like Jürgen Habermas, Karl-Otto

Apel, and Otto Pöggeler. Oscar Becker, whom she labels "a completely doubtful case," is referred to by Gadamer as "a great scholar." But when she brings up Becker's authoritarianism and anti-Semitism, Gadamer has to say that he disagreed with him even at that time. Still, he says she needs to make a distinction between Becker's theories about race in general during the '20s and Hitler's anti-Semitism. She says, well, they combine all too easily with anti-Semitism. This "fellow traveler" thinking, as we could call it, draws an angry retort from Gadamer: "We intellectuals regarded anti-Semites like Werner Butzbach as crazy. For you to act as if the philosophers would have played some kind of role in this anti-Semitism—you just can't do that!" The fact that Becker looked for differentiating characteristics among the races of the world does not make him an anti-Semite.

In reply she says she certainly does indeed think that within the humanities and social sciences "philosophers were a thread in the whole fabric." This belief goes to the heart of the dispute and is in fact the reason she is interviewing Gadamer. Her assumption is that philosophers were highly influential people who either through opportunism or fear entered into collaboration with the Third Reich. Gadamer replies that writers and poets were much more influential at the time because they reached more people. Furthermore, Gadamer replies on behalf of his liberal intellectual colleagues that "none of us gave lectures about a National-Socialistic worldview. None of us talked from the lectern about race. I would not even assume this about Becker!" Gadamer, for his part, was just teaching ancient Greek philosophy and Plato. But she picks up on this and asks whether it was true that "philosophers also suddenly interpreted Plato in such a way that the state Plato imagined became a model for the National Socialist state?" Gadamer replies, "You are vastly underestimating the intelligence of us professors of philosophy!" Yes, he concedes, for a brief moment at the beginning there was one person named Feder who tried to introduce this into the Nazi platform but the Nazis were not interested in it (a footnote on Feder points out that already in late 1933 he was "shoved off to an honorary professorship in Berlin"). At the time, Gadamer says, the analogy of Hitler's Third Reich to a Platonic utopia made philosophers laugh scornfully. He asks: "What do you think of us?"—i.e., how stupid do you think we are? She suddenly asks to drop the subject, but he follows up with the question, "Do you really think we philosophers took seriously all that nonsense in relation to Plato?"

Cornered, she counters by changing the subject to something more personal and more apparently incriminating: his signature on the Appeal for a Reichstag Election and a Vote of the People in 1933. Gadamer explains the presence of his signature on this document by supplying the background context: a public meeting in Marburg in which "we were publicly asked if anyone at all was against it, and nobody had the courage to say yes. Why? *Because that would have meant emigration.* That was how significant it was whether one signed onto this call." This signature, then, was not a voluntary and enthusiastic gesture but a coerced public vote laden with dire consequences if he did not sign. He signed it as did many Jewish colleagues. Yes, she said, but when you signed up for that teachers' camp, certainly that was voluntary! But according to a 1934 law (see note 19 of that conversation), "permission by the state to teach was made dependent on serving probation in a community camp" such as this. At the time, Gadamer and his wife and daughter were in desperate financial straits. He saw this as the only way of getting a job without joining the Party. His dilemma, as he states it, was: "How can I hold out against the opposition of the Party and at the same time not commit a breach of faith with my Jewish friends? I said to myself, 'I will go voluntarily into one of these camps. Maybe it will help me.' And it did. Not that I stated there that I was a supporter of the Nazis." That was not expected. The camp was for non-Party teachers. It was the minimum he could do and still get a job. For Gadamer, it meant personal connections and the possibility of employment; it gave the appearance of cooperation without the reality. As it happened, he was befriended by the leader of the camp, a certain Count Gleispach, who was previously mayor of Vienna, and Gleispach later pulled strings in Berlin to have Gadamer called to Leipzig. But after he was appointed professor in Leipzig, Gadamer declined to work on the Nazi Ancestral Heritage Project on the basis that "I don't have any time."

His years at Leipzig, like those of most intellectuals, were a matter of biding time and living by the motto *Et illud transit*—this too will pass (also a famous saying of the Muslim poet Rumi). Gadamer followed

Theodor Litt in seeing this as an "inner emigration." When von Westernhagen asks him, "Would you see yourself as a case of inner emigration?" his answer is: "We all were!" But what about the project of "The Humanities and the War Effort," where professors joined in the war effort, she asks. Again, there is more to understand: This was an effort to rectify the imbalance whereby the flow of university funds was going into the natural sciences, while the humanities received virtually nothing. Actually this was a stroke of genius, Gadamer said. It worked, and funds flowed into creating translators, which "saved an infinite number of lives," and it organized other projects which created exemptions for the humanists who would otherwise have been drafted and gone straight to the front. The result was many bright young scholars who survived the Second World War and went on to lead fruitful professional lives. Again, behind the mask of participation in the war effort was the motive of saving men from military service. Gadamer's personal strategy was to be pleasant to the Nazis, to smile, to go along, and thus win exemption from something worse. This was his survival strategy in a police state: not overtly shunning the Nazis but rather remaining friends with Nazi colleagues and respecting them for their work, not their politics. He avoided the subject of politics. "My cleverness lay in taking seriously the colleagues who were Nazis but who were also at the same time genuine, rational scholars." That is how he got to Leipzig, he told her, and that is how he was able to remain at Leipzig. His closest colleagues at Marburg were Jewish, and he helped them all he could. He kept a Jewish colleague (Erich Frank) in his house in Marburg, he remained in communication with Karl Löwith and many other friends during the war, and once he made the move to Frankfurt and Heidelberg after the war, he was able to help restore them to their previous positions.

As this conversation makes clear, Gadamer went along when he had to, and even attended an orientation camp that was a condition for gaining any professorship position in Germany, but he certainly was not an "ideological power of Fascism." He created no fascist theory or ideology; he kept his lectures free of references to the Nazis. He did not shun his Nazi colleagues but instead respected them, when he could, for their work. His doctoral specializations from the 1920s in Plato and classical philology were, in the 1930s, not an effort to please the Nazis; rather they were a retreat, his cover, and his title became his excuse for not participating in distasteful projects. Berve, a colleague in classical philology and the rector of Leipzig, saved him several times from being purged, and in the end he was one of those who survived the nightmare. At no time, whether at the beginning, middle, or end of the Third Reich, did he embrace National Socialism, and certainly he was not an ideologist of National Socialism. In my view, this interview may be seen as Gadamer's rebuttal of the charges and innuendos in Orozco's attempted exposé of Gadamer and also Richard Wolin's recent effort to discredit Gadamer.[52] It is a suitable and timely final conversation for this volume.

Endnote Protocol

In these conversations, where the interlocutor or German editor has added citations in the text or endnote information, these have all been retained. The present translator has also provided the reader with references to English translations, where available. The reader can assume that all such information on English translations of Gadamer's writings has been added by the translator. Further information that has been supplied by the translator, either in the text or in the notes, is indicated by square brackets, if inserted into an existing note, or by "trans. note" in the case of complete endnotes by the translator. In the text of the conversations, parenthetical citations of Gadamer's writings refer to the standard German edition of the collected works in ten volumes, *Gesammelte Werke*. The *Gesammelte Werke*, abbreviated *GW*, were published between 1985 and 1995 by J. C. B. Mohr (Paul Siebeck). Gadamer's masterwork, *Wahrheit und Methode*, is the first volume of the collected works, so it will be cited as "*GW* 1," for example *GW* 1(1986): 12–14. Where the year of publication of a work has been previously given, it will generally be omitted: "*GW* 1:12–14." The full publication data for this volume is: Hans-Georg Gadamer, *Gesammelte Werke*, vol. 1: *Hermeneutik I: Wahrheit und Methode: Grundzüge einer philosophischen Hermeneutik* (Tübingen: J. C. B. Mohr [Paul Siebeck], 1986). (The subtitle, which may be translated as *Elements of a Philosophical Hermeneutics*, is omitted in the English translation and in the revised translation.) The collected works will usually be cited when referring to this or any other work of Gadamer, rather than the earlier publication, since this is the authorially revised final text and is easier to access. If an English translation is available and known to the translator, he has supplied it. References to the English translation of Gadamer's *Truth and Method* are to the revised edition. The first translation of *Truth and Method* appeared in 1975, by British scholars Garrett Barden and John Cumming (with their names omitted from the title page) and published by Sheed and Ward in London and Seabury Press in New York. Gathering from Gadamer scholars a large number of suggested alternative renderings to those in the first edition, American Gadamer scholars Joel Weinsheimer and Donald G. Marshall published a cleaned-up version of the earlier translation with Crossroad Publishers of New York in 1989. This revised edition corrected many of the more egregious translation errors. In the present book, all citations of German texts by any author have been newly rendered by this translator, but page references to the English translation, where available, have been supplied as a courtesy to the reader and previous translator.

Acknowledgments

A number of persons deserve my thanks for their help in preparing this volume. Carsten Dutt answered many questions about specific passages and also reviewed, line by line, my translation of his three interviews. Professor Gadamer provided details on citations in the Dutt interviews which had been taken for granted for a German audience, but which called for a more detailed footnote for English-speaking readers. I also thank Jean Grondin for his suggestion of additional interviews that could be included in this volume. My valued colleague Meredith Cargill went over the text of the interviews and made many rhetorical suggestions for its improvement. My draft translations of the three Dutt conversations were presented to the Central Illinois Philosophers Group, who offered many concrete suggestions for their improvement. These have been incorporated into the present translation. I wish especially to mention in that group, José Arcé, Harry Berman, Piotr Boltuc, Meredith Cargill, Bernd Estabrook, Royce Jones, Robert Kunath, Marcia Salner, Larry Shiner, and Peter Wenz. I want to thank MacMurray College for continuing to provide me with an office after my retirement, and librarians Mary Ellen Blackston, Mary Jo Thomas, and Penelope Mitchell for unfailing assistance. I thank my son, Kent Palmer, instructor of computer science at MacMurray College, for his technical help. For bibliographical support, I thank the eminent Japanese scholar Etsuro Makita, whose *Gadamer-Bibliographie*[53] was indispensable in providing accurate details for my citations and for the bibliographical appendices of Gadamer's writings in English. Finally, I thank my editor at Yale University Press, Jeffrey Schier, for many valuable corrections.

I wish to thank the C. Winter Universtätsverlag, Heidelberg, for permission to translate *Hermeneutik-Ästhetik-Praktische Philosophie: Hans-Georg Gadamer im Gespräch* (1993, rev. 1994); the Verlag J. B. Metzler, publisher of the *Internationale Zeitschrift für Philosophie*, for permission to use "Die Griechen, unsere Lehrer: Ein Gespräch mit Glenn W. Most," from Heft 1, Theme: "Antike und Gegenwart" (1994), pp. 139–149; the *Journal of the British Society for Phenomenology* for permission to republish "A Conversation with Hans-Georg Gadamer," Alfons Grieder's translation into English of his 1992 interview with Gadamer, vol. 26, no. 2 (1995): pp. 116–126; and Argument Verlag for permission to translate and publish "Hans-Georg Gadamer im Gespräch mit Dörte von Westernhagen: 'die wirklichen Nazis hatten doch gar kein Interesse an uns'" from *Das Argument: Zeitschrift für Philosophie und Sozialwissenschaften* 32nd year, issue 182, no. 4 (July–August 1990): 543–555.

PART I

GADAMER
IN CONVERSATION WITH
CARSTEN DUTT

PREFACE

TO PART I

The three conversations in this section, hermeneutics, aesthetics, and practical philosophy, transcribed with some slight reworking, are conversations that I had with Professor Gadamer at the beginning of 1993. In editing the text for publication I have added bibliographical citations in the conversations and a few endnotes.[1]

Central to the first of the conversations, on hermeneutics, is Gadamer's discussion of understanding in the humanities and social sciences [*Geisteswissenschaften*]. The general thesis of his hermeneutical philosophy, that effective history and the structure of application radically condition the hermeneutic process, makes us more aware of the reflexive dimension in all undertakings in the humanities and social sciences. It is in no way appropriate, Gadamer claims, to describe the process of preserving the world that has been transmitted to us in our heritage as if this were an activity of purely antiquarian research or of the mastery of a certain subject matter through methods. The true starting point and the proper approach to the relevance of our heritage lies in the questioning that it directs to us. For this reason Gadamer speaks in terms of a conversation with our heritage, a conversation in which our interpretation of it causes us to have a new and broader understanding of ourselves.

The point that takes shape at the end of this first conversation is that the interaction we have with our heritage takes place in a world of conversation—that is, in a hermeneutic universe. In this universe we can pursue our lives successfully only if we are able to achieve an understanding of and with other persons, and the way to accomplish this is for each person to picture herself or himself as the other person in a conversation. The all-encompassing theme in this first section is hermeneutic philosophy, a philosophy that takes the medium of language as its starting point and sees our form of life as constituted by communication.

In the second conversation a number of questions are posed on the topic of a hermeneutical *aesthetics*. Unlike the first conversation, where Gadamer's main work, *Truth and Method*, was the reference text, the focus here is on his later work. What becomes clear in these writings is that when one undertakes to describe the process of uncovering the orientation of meaning—*Sinnorientierung*—of a work of art, which is the basic movement of understanding in aesthetic experience, one cannot equate aesthetic understanding with non-aesthetic understanding. They are not interchangeable. Indeed, a central task that is opened up by the field of hermeneutical aesthetics is to investigate the processes of understanding which are particularly involved in the encounter with artwork. In contrast to the structure of appropriating a meaning in pragmatic contexts, where ultimately the vehicle of the meaning is swallowed up in the process of overcoming whatever difficulties may obstruct a successful construction of meaning, the understanding of a work of art, through the reading either of an image or of an eminent text, knows no such end result. "In the concrete existence of the work, our understanding experiences the unfathomable depths of its meaning."

The third conversation, which appeared in slightly shortened form in Heidelberg's newspaper, the *Rhein-Neckar-Zeitung*, in connection with Gadamer's ninety-third birthday on February 11, 1993, deals with questions of practical philosophy, and its main insight is expressed in the concept of a solidarity that exists among human beings. Practical philosophy, which as ethics inquires into "the good," can only do its work as the self-

clarification of a concrete *ethos:* "We are not here trying to invent a solidarity but to make ourselves conscious of it."

Gadamer has repeatedly explained that he understands the basic task
of philosophy in this way: "To philosophize . . . is to lead philosophy,
whose language is alienated from its originary meaning in speech, back
to the commonalities which sustain our speaking."[2]

This intention is also well shown by the following: Whether Gadamer
is speaking about the nature of experience, about conversation, about
coming to an understanding in conversation, about reading, or about the
meaning of the word "classic" in its applied sense, his concepts are always
wrested from the hermeneutical resources of the life-world and clarified
on the basis of the solidarity of our understanding of it outside of all specialized discourse.

I would like to thank Professor Gadamer for his readiness to enter
into these conversations, and for his friendly patience in helping to eval-
uate the considerable materials covered in the transcribed tape-record-
ings of them.

Carsten Dutt
Heidelberg, Easter 1993

1

HERMENEUTICS

D U T T : Professor Gadamer, the term "hermeneutics," generally associated with your path of thinking, was not originally a philosophical term. When one looks up "hermeneutics" in a dictionary, the definition is basically "the art of interpretation" [*Auslegungskunst* art of explication] or "a teaching about interpretation" [*Auslegungslehre*]. When hermeneutics is defined in this way, it has a long history. So could I first ask you to discuss this history, which can be called the prehistory of philosophical hermeneutics?

G A D A M E R : If one goes back to the original meaning of the Greek term *hermeneia*, and "hermeneutics" as meaning translation and interpretation, this depicts quite clearly the situation in which early Christianity found itself in relation to Greek philosophy, and how Augustine in the *De Doctrina Christiana* tried to translate into conceptual terms the way one was to speak of the Christian message. *Homo timens Deum, voluntatem eius in Scripturis sanctis diligenter inquirit*[1] [Man, fear God and diligently inquire into the Scriptures]. You know this famous text. Now this idea [of translating Scripture into conceptual terms, as Augustine

36

did] was accomplished in a different form by the Scholastics in the Middle Ages through their wonderful intellectual achievement in receiving and making use of Aristotelian metaphysics. But only with Luther and, above all, Melanchthon was hermeneutics accorded a new function in relation to reading the Bible, a function they described in terms of the tools provided by Aristotelian rhetoric. With this step, hermeneutics [as the discipline of interpreting Scripture with the help of rhetorical principles] took its place alongside the explication of the law in the new jurisprudence of the time. This marks a clear boundary that separates hermeneutics from the form taken by modern science with its mathematical development. With the spread of a humanistic reading-culture, hermeneutics was developed as an aid to the interpreter in understanding sentences and texts as such.

In the Romantic era Schleiermacher and Friedrich Schlegel showed that all understanding is always already interpretation [*Auslegung*, explication]. You will recall that previously, in the eighteenth century, one had distinguished the *subtilitas intelligendi*, power of understanding, from *subtilitas explicandi*, the power of interpretation. Romanticism, however, recognized the unity of these two moments in the process, and by virtue of this the universal role of language. In other words, one should not imagine that interpretive concepts only enter into one's understanding subsequently, as if one drew them out of a linguistic storeroom, so to speak, and applied them as needed to the "thing to be understood." Such a conception is completely wrong, and there is really nobody today who holds it. No, understanding does not reach out and take hold of language; it is carried out within language.

Then, in our century, it was Heidegger who took the decisive step in thought, following the lead of Dilthey. Heidegger asserted that in all understanding there is a third moment involved in the process: that of *understanding oneself—Sich selbst-Verstehen*; this is a kind of application, which in the era of German pietism [eighteenth century] was called the *subtilitas applicandi*. Following the lead of Heidegger, I myself used this third moment in order to demonstrate the limits of the scientific concept of method. For the hermeneutic process involves not only the moments of understanding and of interpretation but also the moment of application; that is to say, understanding oneself is a part of this process. Now I am willing to admit that the concept of *Applikation*, a concept that is accidental and offered itself historically, is artificial and misleading. But I certainly had not anticipated that one could think that, according to it, understanding should be applied to something else. No, I mean that it is to be applied to oneself.

D U T T : Along with the moment of application contained in all understanding you have now indicated an important point which interests me very much and which I would like to pursue further. Although we have agreed to speak about some of the results of your work, could we perhaps take a moment to discuss your presuppositions? You yourself have mentioned your teacher, Martin Heidegger. In the history of hermeneutics, the "hermeneutics of facticity,"[2] which Heidegger developed within his ontological standpoint of questioning, signifies an innovation that has been foundational for your own approach. The writing of the history of philosophy quite legitimately takes away the novelty of the sudden appearance of the new by identifying all the preliminary stages and advance indications. This holds true in the case of Heidegger also, for whom Dilthey is the most important of the names one could suggest in relation to hermeneutics. You yourself have also just mentioned him. Could I now perhaps link my question about Heidegger's hermeneutics of facticity with the question of your own relationship to Dilthey's analyses of understanding?

G A D A M E R : The debate in hermeneutics that is going on today is, as a matter of fact, dominated by the question of Dilthey and his influence. How are we to assess this influence in relation to the development of hermeneutical philosophy? Well, certainly Dilthey's work mediated essential stimuli to the thinking of the young Heidegger, and he used these to further develop and reshape Husserlian phenomenology. But what Dilthey was dealing with was psychology. Only after Heidegger had developed a hermeneutics of facticity—that is to say, a hermeneutics of the human being as concretely existing here and now—and published this in *Being and Time* in 1927 did the Dilthey school through Georg Misch begin to be interested in the development of hermeneutics.[3]

Since that time people have even gone so far as to call hermeneutics the true *koine* [common language] of philosophizing in our time. Now why is it that hermeneutics came to have such a special meaning in Heidegger—although even he later rejected this designation? My answer is: that Heidegger and only Heidegger opened our eyes to the fact that what we were dealing with here is *the concept of being*. Certainly Heidegger would not have been led to see Being in the horizon of time and, on the basis of the movement of human existing, to think that the human being projected its future and came from out of its heritage, without the stimuli he received from Dilthey, from Bergson, and from Aristotle. So Heidegger designated understanding as an *existentiale*; that is, as a categorical and basic determinant of our being-in-the-world. When we see the matter from this standpoint, we realize that Heidegger did not have as his aim either a theory of the humanities and social sciences [*Geisteswissenschaften*]⁴ or a critique of historical reason, which were the tasks Dilthey had posed for himself.

Of course, the task still remained of taking the philosophical awakening of Heidegger and applying it to the *Geisteswissenschaften* and to show its validity there. This is the task to which I have tried to contribute. What I tried to do, following Heidegger, was to see the linguisticality of human beings not just in terms of the subjectivity of consciousness and the capacity for language in that consciousness, as German idealism and Humboldt had done. Instead, I moved the idea of conversation to the very center of hermeneutics. Perhaps a phrase from Hölderlin will make clear to you what kind of turn this move involved. Because Heidegger could no longer accept the dialectical reconciliation with Christianity that had marked the whole post-Hegelian epoch, he sought the Word through Hölderlin, whose words "Seit ein Gespräch wir sind/Und hören können voneinander" [Since we are a conversation/And can hear one another] inspired him. Now Heidegger had understood this as the conversation of human beings with the gods.⁵ Perhaps correctly so. But the hermeneutic turn, which is grounded in the linguisticality of the human being, at least also includes us in Hölderlin's "one another," and at the same time it contains the idea that we as human beings have to learn from each other. We do not need just to hear one another but to *listen to* one another. Only when this happens is there understanding.

D U T T : In your masterwork *Truth and Method* of 1960, both strands of your work that are indebted to Heidegger are represented: your discussion of understanding in the humanities and social sciences in the second part and in the third part of that work, your grounding of hermeneutics in a theory of language. The first part of your book developed a hermeneutical perspective on the experience of art. With your permission, I would like to put this general structure aside and take up the part that has found the greatest international resonance, that is, the part on the humanities and social sciences. In relation to this the introduction to *Truth and Method* announces that it will undertake "the quest for an understanding of what the humanities and social sciences [*Geisteswissenschaften*] really are beyond their own methodological self-awareness and take up what links them with the totality of our experience of the world" (*GW* 1: 3/*TM* xxiii). Could you explain what change of perspective you are suggesting? How would it differ from the present methodological thematization of these disciplines?

GADAMER: The term "method" in the title of my book already points toward this difference. I was not trying to do what Betti in his debate with Croce and Gentile tried to do, namely, to extend the methods originally belonging to theological and juristic hermeneutics into other disciplines in order to ensure that the concept of method had the widest possible scope of application; no, on the contrary, what I sought to show was that the concept of method was not an appropriate way of achieving legitimation in the humanities and social sciences. What is involved is not just a matter of using certain procedures to deal with a certain region of objects. The humanities and social sciences, whose honor I am trying to defend by offering a more appropriate theoretical justification, really belong in the same line of succession, and have the same heritage as philosophy. They may be distinguished from the natural sciences not only through their ways of proceeding but also through the preliminary relationship they have to their subject matter; that is, through their participation in the heritage that they renew and articulate for us again and again. This is the reason I have suggested that the ideal of objective knowledge which dominates our concepts of knowledge, science, and truth, needs to be supplemented by the ideal of sharing in something, of participation. We participate in the essential expressions of human experience that have been developed in our artistic, religious, and historical tradition—and not only in ours but in all cultures; this possible participation is the true criterion for the wealth or the poverty of what we produce in our humanities and social sciences. One could express this in another way by saying that philosophy is deeply embedded in all the humanities and social sciences, but this is never completely conceptualized.

D U T T : Your critics have seen in your argument a rejection of methodology in general. Some of them have interpreted the title of your book to mean "truth versus method."[6]

G A D A M E R : This interpretation conveys the one-sided impression that I think there are no methods in the humanities and social sciences. Of course there are methods, and certainly one must learn them and apply them. But I would say that the fact that we are able to apply certain methods to certain objects does not establish *why* we are pursuing knowledge in the humanities and social sciences. To me it seems self-evident that in the natural sciences one pursues knowledge ultimately because through them one can stand on one's own feet: one can orient oneself and through measurement, reckoning, and construction eventually gain control of the surrounding world. By doing this we can—at least this is their intention—live better and survive better than if we just confronted a nature that is indifferent to us. But in the humanities and social sciences [*Geisteswissenschaften*] there can be nothing like such ruling over the historical world. The humanities and social sciences bring something different into our lives through their form of participation in what has been handed down to us, something that is not knowledge for the sake of control [*Herrschaftswissen*[7]], yet it is no less important. We customarily call it "culture."

D U T T : What you are talking about is a thinking that goes way beyond the methodological self-understanding of the humanistic [*geisteswissenschaftlichen*] disciplines . . .

G A D A M E R : . . . to their philosophical content. Which relativizes the concept of method but does not cancel it out.

D U T T : This clarification is important.

G A D A M E R : Of course, otherwise we are faced with false alternatives. As tools, methods are always good to have. But one must understand where these can be fruitfully used. Methodical sterility is a generally known phenomenon. Every once in a while, for instance, we find tried and true or merely fashionable methods applied in a field where they are simply unproductive. What does the truly productive researcher do? What does an Ernst Robert Curtius or a Leo Spitzer do? Are they creative because they have mastered the methods in that field? Applying method is what the person does who never finds out anything new, who never brings to light an interpretation that has revelatory power. No, it is not their mastery of methods but their hermeneutical imagination that distinguishes truly productive researchers. And what is hermeneutical imagination? It is a sense of the questionableness of something and what this requires of us.

By the way, the question of whether there is also a hermeneutics appropriate to the natural sciences needs to be taken seriously. In the philosophy of science since Thomas Kuhn this point has been widely discussed. I think this is above all because natural scientific methods do not show us how to apply the results of natural scientific work to the practice of living life in a rational way. As Kant has said: There is no rule for how one learns to apply the rules correctly.

D U T T : Indeed, one finds a hermeneutic structure in the way the fields of the natural sciences are formed.

G A D A M E R : Of course! And you can even go farther and pose the question: What is "the given," anyway, which research in the natural sciences takes as the secure foundation on which it goes its way? Does something [like "the given"] ever stand immediately before our eyes entirely unmediated by anything? Or is it not the case that even what one sees as the movement of a pointer [on a gauge] or what appears under a microscope is always the result of that mediation which we call *understanding?* In this connection, the lesson we learned in the history of philosophy is well known. I mean the collapse of the theory of protocol sentences. In the realm of the natural sciences, also, in my opinion, in the theory of knowledge one cannot avoid the hermeneutical criticism that "the given" cannot be separated from understanding. Even in all protocol-formulating procedures, even in so-called perception itself, the hermeneutic understanding of something-as-something is still operative.

D U T T : Let's talk about the elements in your discussion of understanding in the humanities and social sciences that have provoked objections. I am thinking especially of your introduction of the concept of prejudgment or prejudice [*Vorurteil*] as something positive, and linked with this your critique of the epistemological discourse of the Enlightenment.

Or more precisely, a particular strand of Enlightenment epistemology. Could you straighten this out?

GADAMER: Yes. The radical Enlightenment declared war on all prejudgments whatever. That was its emotional appeal, its *pathos*, so to speak. And by means of this, it accomplished a kind of liberation, an emancipation of the mind. But if one goes on from this to draw the conclusion that one can become transparent to oneself, that one can become sovereign in one's thinking and action, then one is mistaken. No one knows himself or herself [*Niemand kennt sich selbst*]. We always already have a certain character; no one is a blank sheet of paper. Communication with one's mother begins long before any speaking at all; as we know today, it begins already in the mother's body. In every other respect, too, we know that nobody really is fully aware of the things that cause him or her to become who he or she is. We are not just stamped by our "genes" but also by the socialization through which we are in a position to gain access to our world and to the traditions in which we exist. These characteristics imprinted on our minds open up our horizons, and of course also limit them. But it is only through them that we have a horizon at all and are able to encounter something that broadens our horizon.

DUTT: Once again you are upsetting the order of my list of questions! The concept of horizons already takes us into your description of the way understanding is carried out: that is, to your model of the fusion of horizons. But I would like to linger a bit longer with the issue of prejudgments and with your thesis that because these are unavoidable in the practice of knowing, and total self-enlightenment is an illusory claim, then the researcher in the humanities and social sciences is not relieved of the duty of reflecting on his or her expectations or spelling out his or her prejudices.

GADAMER: No, no! Certainly not! Nor does it relieve anyone of the duty to disempower, where possible, prejudices that do not prove to be positive. But it is also possible for prejudgments to play a positive role in understanding!

DUTT: And from the unavoidability of prejudice it follows in your argument that we must rehabilitate their sources; thus the indispensability of authority and tradition. These concepts generate misunderstanding—even after or perhaps precisely because of the so-called change of direction in the social–political discussion here in Germany. In your debate with Habermas, for instance, objections to your chapter in *Truth and Method* on "the rehabilitation of authority and tradition" played an important role. And in your new edition of *Truth and Method* for the collected works you add a commentary note on this matter. But still you did not make any changes in the text itself.

GADAMER: No. Why? Because one can still see in what I have presented that there is something in the argument that has a point. The idea that authority and tradition are something one can appeal to for validation is a pure misunderstanding. Whoever appeals to authority and tradition will have no authority. Period. The same thing goes for prejudgments. Anyone who simply appeals to prejudices is not someone you can talk with. Indeed, a person who is not ready to put his or her own prejudices in question is also someone to whom there is no point in talking. One time, at the beginning of his career, Heidegger made use of the term *Vorurteilsuberlegenheit* [one's superiority over prejudgment] as a corrective measure. This concept includes the capacity for conceding the correctness of the argument of the other person, and in cases where one does not know enough and one has trust in the better knowledge of the other person, one recognizes his or her "authority" in the matter. All our learning is based on this. Good judgment [a positive form of prejudgment] is a faculty one uses in taking action or in claiming to know something, and of course it is not something one acquires through book learning.

DUTT: "People who appear to be sure of their freedom from prejudice, supporting themselves with the objectivity of their procedures and denying their historical conditioning, will experience the violence of the prejudices that rule unchecked as a *vis a tergo* [power operating behind one's back] (*GW* 1: 366/*TM* 360).

GADAMER: That's right!

DUTT: Yes, that is a quote from *Truth and Method*—

GADAMER: Yes, I know.

DUTT: —a quotation that seems to me especially well suited to clarifying your offer here to "enlighten" us about your ideas—if, given the present context, I may use this word! Your true target is really a form of historical consciousness which has been the guiding consciousness of the modern humanities and social sciences, insofar as its insight into the historicity of its objects has been paired with a blindness to its own inextricable involvement in that history.

G A D A M E R : Yes, this is historical objectivism, the naïveté of a faith in method, into which anyone falls who thinks that in understanding one is able to leave oneself out.

D U T T : You write, "One must move away from a historical thinking that is badly understood, and appeal for a better understanding of what such thinking means. A thinking that is genuinely historical must think its own historicity along with whatever it thinks" (*GW* 1: 304 ff./ *TM* 299). Accordingly, the task of philosophical hermeneutics "is to demonstrate the reality of history existent *in understanding itself.*" This you call the "principle of effective history" [*Wirkungsgeschichte*] and your thesis reads: "Understanding, by its very nature . . . is an occurrence in which history is operative" (*GW* 1: 305/*TM* 299–300).

G A D A M E R : Yes, indeed! Historical consciousness must learn to understand itself better and to recognize that its interpretive [*hermeneutische*] efforts are constantly co-determined by an effective-historical factor. We stand in traditions, whether we know these traditions or not; that is, whether we are conscious of these or are so arrogant as to think we can begin without presuppositions—none of this changes the way traditions are working on us and in our understanding.

D U T T : We have now been living for some two hundred years in an ongoing but very gradual process of emancipation from traditions—

G A D A M E R : —My thesis of the conditionedness of all understanding by history operating in it does not contradict this! You need to be on guard against false connotations associated with the word "tradition."[8] Tradition is not something which one knows as one's own heritage [*Herkunft*] in such a way that one can accept or reject it. I see no reason not to emphasize the factor of tradition which is in play [or at work] in all understanding, as something that applies even in the present day. The democratic tradition of Germany, for instance, although still young, certainly has a considerable effect on the interpretive [*hermeneutische*] horizon of our research projects in history. One could demonstrate this with numerous other examples. No, people who believe they have freed themselves from their interwovenness into their effective history [*Wirkungsgeschichte*] are simply mistaken.

D U T T : In fact, you speak in *Truth and Method* not only of this ef-fective-historical interconnectedness but also of a historically effective reflection, that is, a kind of effective-historical consciousness which needs to be developed in the *Geisteswissenschaften* [humanities and social sci-ences].

G A D A M E R : Yes, and one can certainly say that one of the greatest challenges Heidegger faced in accepting the whole of my work was that I used the term *consciousness*. Despite the fact that I said very plainly in *Truth and Method* that the consciousness in which history is operative [the *wirkungsgeschichtliches Bewußtsein* often translated as the effective historical consciousness] was more *Sein* [Being] than *Bewußtsein* [con-sciousness]. In living one always finds oneself already in a situation that is conditioned by effective history. In the concept of situation, I still firmly hold the view that one can never by means of reflection place oneself in an externalized relation to one's situation. This does not mean that schol-ars in the humanities and social sciences do not have the task of using their powers to develop a consciousness of their own situation, the situa-tion in which they stand over against the tradition that they are trying to understand. Quite the contrary! In every genuine effort at research one needs to work out a consciousness of one's hermeneutical situation. Only in this way can one shed light on the basis of one's interests in it and on what supports one's standpoint of questioning. And of course one still must confess the endlessness of this task. Full enlightenment about one's own interests in questioning is not attainable. There is always something remaining that one does not realize. In any case, however, one needs to get away from objectivist naïveté and destroy the illusion of a truth that is separate from the standpoint of the one doing the understanding.

The effective-historical consciousness knows that that which shows it-self as the object of investigation is not an "object" which the progress of research will somehow eventually unveil *in seinem Ansichseins* [in its being as it is in itself]. Rather, with a historical phenomenon—a picture, a text, a political or social event—one is able to see one's own self in the other, in the sense that through it one learns to comprehend oneself better. Of course, I do not deny the tension that characterizes the modern humani-ties and social sciences. The achievement of an historical consciousness is not a covering over of the tension between past and present by hasty comparisons; it is a consciousness that recognizes the otherness of the past. But in knowing this otherness it knows only half. To the whole belongs the functioning of history in consciousness. The hermeneutical situation of the researcher is to stand always between strangeness and familiarity, between the mere objectivity of what has been handed down to us and the fact of our belonging to that heritage. In other words, knowledge in the humanities and social sciences always has something of self-knowledge in it. This kind of application can never be taken away.

D U T T : Perhaps now is the right time take up the concept of application, which I tried to avoid a while back. The large chapter you dedicate to it attempts to have application, which is recognized as a generic task in theological and juristic hermeneutics, also be recognized in the humanistic disciplines as the basic hermeneutical problem. The correcting of the [objectivist] "historical consciousness" through one in which history is always already at work takes place as a correction of the hermeneutics of "reconstruction" [of the past]. You show that when historians and philologists speak in terms of reconstruction of the past, there is still always lurking in it a moment of application. How can this moment best be demonstrated?

G A D A M E R : Well, as I said at the beginning of our conversation, what we are dealing with here is not the taking of something that was first understood in itself and then "applying" it subsequently to something else; rather, application is involved in the first real reaching of an understanding of a matter by the person who is seeking to understand it. In all understanding an application occurs, such that the person who is understanding is himself or herself *right there* in the understood meaning. He or she *belongs to* the subject-matter that he or she is understanding.

D U T T : Could you perhaps clarify this ["belonging to"] with an example? What does this look like in the humanities and social sciences, say in literature or history? The hermeneutical practice in these disciplines as a rule seems not to have the proper application-intentions . . .

G A D A M E R : This is not what I mean, either! I am certainly not speaking about hermeneutic practice as if it were always guided by an "intention to apply." Application is an *implicit* moment in all understanding; it does not at all conflict with genuine obligation to have scientific rigor. One does not accomplish application by taking some excerpt from the tradition and then making some doubtful "application" of it; rather, application takes place in order for one to understand it at all! In order to grasp the meaning that some piece of our tradition [*Überlieferungsaus-schnitt*] has, one must relate it to the concrete hermeneutical situation in which one finds oneself. Everyone who understands something understands himself or herself in it. The researcher, too. Then and today are mediated in the researcher's work—the historical heritage with which he or she is dealing is mediated through his or her own present time.

D U T T : But doesn't that exclude the idea that there can ever be a final and conclusive understanding of that particular piece of our heritage?

G A D A M E R : Every encounter with what has come down to us in history is a historically different encounter. As I have formulated this point in *Truth and Method* one understands differently when one understands at all.[9]

D U T T : This also reinforces your characterization of the process of understanding as a fusion of horizons. Where two horizons fuse, something arises that did not exist before.

G A D A M E R : Yes, and this happens continuously. Horizons are not rigid but mobile; they are in motion because our prejudgments are constantly put to the test. This happens in every encounter with what has come down to us, also.

D U T T : Now, as you yourself emphasize, one of the special features of the fusion of horizons, when one carries it out under the restrictions of scientific rigor, is that it contains an element of the hermeneutics of reconstruction: a projection of the historical horizon of the subject-matter which the researcher, whether philologist or historian, is investigating. Here, of course, you also go on to speak of "a phase in the carrying out of understanding" that is not fixed and established but rather "is brought in from your own present horizon of understanding" (*GW* 1: 312/*TM* 307).

G A D A M E R : Quite right! A historically well-schooled interpreter profiles the horizon of that which has come down to him or her against that of his or her own time-horizon, but actually his understanding already includes a mediation of both horizons. His or her projecting of the historical horizon that is profiled against the horizon of the present is *aufgehoben* [both annulled and taken up into a higher form] in understanding, which signifies the gaining of a new historical horizon.

D U T T : You have compared the form in which the fusion of horizons takes place with the form of a conversation. Just as when two partners in a conversation seek to reach an understanding about a topic, so also between the philologist and his text, between the historian and what he or she is researching, a communication, a hermeneutic conversation, takes place. This analogy of yours has not found universal acceptance. In particular, your description of how this conversation arises has irritated some people in that you see it as initiated *from the side of the tradition*, a position which is perfectly consistent within the framework of the concept of effective history. Nevertheless, this has been taken to be a stylizing that attributes to tradition false action-predicates. Tradition is elevated into the position of a subject.

G A D A M E R : Well, I believe I have shown that, in understanding, a "subject" does not stand over against an "object" or a world of objects. Rather something plays back and forth between the human being and that which he or she encounters in the world. So one of the most essential experiences a human being can have is that another person comes to know him or her better. This means, however, that we must take the encounter with the other person seriously, because there is always something about which we are not correct and are not justified in maintaining. Through an encounter with the other we are lifted above the narrow confines of our own knowledge. A new horizon is disclosed that opens onto what was unknown to us. In every genuine conversation this happens. We come closer to the truth because we do not exist by ourselves. And, you ask, why is the encounter with what has come down to us and in which something is said to us also a conversation? It is a conversation because what comes to meet us from the tradition poses a question to us that we have to answer. Something from the tradition *addresses* us—a work of art is an [historical] event which we understand all at once: this encounter engages us the same way a partner in a conversation does.

D U T T : But this is the very thing that has not been persuasive to everyone: the idea that *what is handed down poses questions to us*. Certainly that is the point of your chapter on question and answer, a point which you emphasize once again at the end of your book. There you write, "What seems to be the thesis-like beginning of the interpretation is in reality already an answer, and like every answer the sense of an interpretation has been determined through the question that is posed. *The dialectic of question and answer is already prefigured in the dialectic of interpretation. This is what determines understanding as an event"* (*GW* 1: 476/ *TM* 472). This thesis, however, brought you into conflict with the self-understanding of some professional interpreters.

G A D A M E R : But that is just the point! How do we come to pose our questions? When we pose them, how do we go about answering them? No problem just falls from heaven. Something awakens our interest—that is really what comes first! At the beginning of every effort to understand is a concern about something: confronted by a question one is to answer, one's knowledge of what one is interpreting is thrown into uncertainty, and this causes one to search for an answer. In order to come up with an answer, the person then begins asking questions. But no one asks questions *von sich aus* [just from oneself]—apropos of nothing. To think otherwise is simply to fall into scientific ideology. No, understanding is not something that takes place at the end of humanistic research about an object, it stands at the beginning and governs the whole process of questioning, step by step.

I must emphasize once again that the *Geisteswissenschaften* [humanities and social sciences] have not attained the distinctive place they hold because they are *Wissenschaften* [sciences]. As sciences, they do not have any better methods than the other "sciences." No, the *Geisteswissenschaften* have attained their respected eminence because in them we repeatedly come to realize something we did not know before, something we have always wanted to know. What they offer has first to be *said to* us and then we respond by saying, "I understand."

D U T T : But what about this "I"? How are you able to retain the "I" in this "I understand"? Some people have complained that under your principle of effective history, the understanding subject becomes for you a mere reflex of tradition, which you have absolutized into a supersubject. Manfred Frank has formulated this objection as follows: "The tradition is [for Gadamer] the mediation of what mediates and what is mediated, but only in and for itself."[10] Under these circumstances, Manfred Frank fears that the claim that is implicit in conversation as the model of understanding and also in the model of the fusion of horizons, namely that in every understanding something new comes into existence, can only be legitimated through some kind of trick. In your thought, he says, tradition becomes a supersubject that is "overpowered by its own riches, so that in the individual blazing up of meaning a virtual infinity of what is interpretable presses to be brought into language."[11]

Now certainly I do not find Manfred Frank's objections persuasive, but I would like to repeat to you one of the questions that he poses in his critique. He asks: If understanding is subject to the workings of history [*Wirkungsgeschichte*], how do you justify the sentence that you yourself have brought into the discussion, namely: "When one understands at all, one understands differently." How do you safeguard and defend this sentence within the framework of your own concepts?

G A D A M E R : My answer is this: *through language.* In the short history of hermeneutics that you asked me to provide earlier, I already alluded to the realization by the romantics that all understanding is interpretation and that understanding is inextricably bound up with language. Part Three of *Truth and Method* concerns itself with the problem of the linguistic character of understanding. As that part of the book tries to demonstrate, when I speak of a hermeneutical conversation with the tradition, with what has come down to us, this is not just a metaphorical manner of speaking but an exact description of how the understanding of the tradition takes place; it is an understanding that takes place in the medium of language. Language is not a supplement of understanding. Understanding and interpretation are always intertwined with each other. Explication in language brings understanding to explicitness; it makes concrete the meaning that comes to be understood in the encounter with what has been handed down to us. The thesis I propose, namely, that in every case this happens in a particular historical situation and that the tradition poses questions and points the way to answers, in no way entails that the tradition is some kind of "supersubject." No, the conversation with the tradition is a genuine conversation, a conversation in which the one who is encountering the word plays an active role. The language of the interpretation is *his or her* language, not just "the language of the text," whose implications of meaning he or she is seeking to unfold. In this respect the interpretation of the tradition, of what has been handed down to us, is never a mere repetition of its words but rather a new creation of the understanding that achieves determinate expression in the words that interpret it.

D U T T : A concept from the older hermeneutical tradition that you yourself have used again and again is that of the *scopus*.

G A D A M E R : Oh yes! This has been a fundamental point in hermeneutics ever since Melanchthon.

D U T T : Whoever wants to understand a text appropriately must ask for its principal intention, the central point of view. The grasp of the *scopus* forms the basis for the endless nuancing work involved in understanding. Now if I had to characterize the *scopus* of the second part of *Truth and Method*, I would say that its basic intention is to describe the *Geisteswissenschaften* not as a component part of the autonomously functioning system of "science," but as a component part of a general world of "experience" that includes both the world of experts and the world of the layperson. Experience is the basic term in your analysis of the effective historical consciousness. In clarifying this concept, you distinguish it very clearly from other philosophical explications of the concept of experience. For example, when Arnold Gehlen talks about the character of experience, his discussion is about how experience selects, arranges, and places things at our disposal and structures them into a system. This set of characteristics stands completely under the rubric of the concept of experience that one finds in the so-called empirical sciences, and indeed Gehlen expressly relates his concept to the exemplary crisis-proof firmness of the natural sciences. In these sciences, only certain kinds of experiences are allowed in, while others, from the very first, are excluded. Elevating this model to a rule of life, Gehlen writes the following about the experienced person: "What is to be allowed into consciousness, there to be worked through, must be steered by it; otherwise one is either an intellectual or a disciple of the Enlightenment."[12] Your concept of experience stands in contrast to this.

G A D A M E R : Yes. Only I would not want to just call it "my" concept of experience! This is the way experience in the *life-world* is lived. The Gehlen counterexample does characterize the matter correctly to the extent that for him, experience is what enables one finally to become an experienced person. But being experienced does not mean that one now knows something once and for all and becomes rigid in this knowledge; rather, one becomes more open to new experiences. A person who is experienced is undogmatic. Experience has the effect of freeing one to be open to experience, as I have said in that chapter on experience—which I do in fact regard as the centerpiece of the whole book.[13] Experience is, I think, the least well known concept in philosophy as a whole, and this is because the so-called sciences of experience [*Erfahrungswissenschaften*] took the experiment as their starting-point and made it a paradigm for experience. These sciences only grant space to an experience if they can obtain from it methodically guaranteed answers to questions. But on the whole, our life is not like this. Our lives are not lived according to scientifically guaranteed programs and secure from crises; rather, we have to undergo our experiences ourselves. This is why I cited the *pathei-mathos* [through suffering learn wisdom] maxim of Aeschylus, in which far more is concealed than the insight that through being injured we become smarter. Aeschylus is showing us our finitude. In our experience we bring nothing to a close; we are constantly learning new things from our experience. And in fact the humanities and social sciences have their special significance in the fact that no experience they deal with can be closed, wrapped up, finished; this I call *die Unabschließbarkeit aller Erfahrung* [the interminability of all experience]. In contrast to the natural sciences, the humanistic disciplines have no methodically "assured" results that we can pass along free of questions. Rather, in the *Geisteswissenschaften* we are constantly learning new things from what has been passed down to us. A genuine readiness for experience goes with this also, an openness to the claim to truth that confronts us in what is handed down to us. So in these disciplines we find something different from just arranging things in historical order. In them we come upon new insights. And that always means, also, that we are released from blindnesses that held us captive.

D U T T : In this connection, I should mention that you have refrained from putting forward a functional thesis that would allocate to the humanities and social sciences a certain goal to reach in our framework of experience. Joachim Ritter, as is well known, did put forward such a functional thesis during the early sixties in an essay that became quite famous. In this essay he described "The Task of the *Geisteswissenschaften* in Modern Society."[14] Ritter saw this task as doing everything possible to make the "historic" vividly present to an industrial society, a society that was in the long term increasingly dominated by the systematic compulsions of natural-scientific and technical-scientific modernization processes and saw the historic as merely historical. The humanities and social sciences, according to Ritter, must compensate for "the palpably real movement in which the old historical possessions we have are being displaced and forgotten"; the humanities and social sciences, then, must rescue and hold onto what "has become remote from present reality." The loss of what has been made remote due to modernization becomes bearable if one still retains a knowledge of it. In providing this knowledge the human sciences are ultimately performing a service for the natural scientific, technical, industrial sector. They help us to react to the losses due to modernization with a "historical sense," and in doing so the social sciences are actually making modernization possible; they are "modernization-enabling"—a conception represented today by Odo Marquard, above all, who got it from Ritter.[15] Now as far as I can see, Professor Gadamer, you have not shown much of a taste for this compensation theorem.

GADAMER: No. The reason I cannot accept the functional determination of the Geisteswissenschaften put forward by Ritter and his followers is that they narrow themselves down to a concept of science and to a historical sense that are defined within this context. This approach is not really appropriate to the subject-matter of the humanities and social sciences. The "historical sense" on which the the Geisteswissenschaften were based in the nineteenth century is not the last word on the subject; rather it represents only a preliminary characterization of today's world of experience and its relation to the tradition. I must confess that in recent years I have not kept track of the individual works of the Ritter school. I am of the opinion, though, that their compensation theorem underestimates the experiential potential of the humanities and social sciences. How are we to know in advance what insights and what understanding and self-understanding the experience of what has come down to us will lead to, and indeed this includes what has come down to us from world cultures, not just the European! Indeed, we in the humanities and social sciences need to accept our worldwide heritage not only in its otherness but also in recognizing the validity of the claim this larger heritage makes on us.

This is to say we must approach it recognizing that it has *something to say to us*. For this we will need openness—but I have already spoken about this. Establishing the humanities and social sciences on a historical basis, however, as we find in Ritter, cannot cause this basic openness to be accepted as valid. In spite of the great accomplishments that of course make him so outstanding, Ritter defines what has come down to us as "the historical." In doing so his thinking remains under the influence of his teacher Heimsoeth. No, the stance of the compensation theorists is not fair to what it means really *to live with* that which comes down to us. The lived experience of encountering what has come down to us is a hermeneutical process—without end and always far beyond all formulas about the sociopolitical functions and goals of the *Geisteswissenschaften*.

D U T T : In contrast to the Ritter school, also, you have not described the humanities and social sciences as exclusively narrative sciences.

G A D A M E R : No, they are not that, either. Of course I myself have worked with the problem of narrativity. In some of my later writings this plays an important role. In the *Geisteswissenschaften* narration does occur, but our heritage is of course also constantly transposed into concepts, and these open up new conceptual horizons. Also, certainly statistics are evaluated, comparisons presented, and texts interpreted. But all this only in order to learn how to comprehend ourselves more adequately. Plato praised the Greek orator Isocrates by saying that there was something like philosophy in his way of thinking: *dianoia* [mathematical reasoning].[16] This also holds with regard to what one calls the "history of philosophy": it interests us because there is *philosophy* in it. I think the point that remains true is this: One must take seriously why I titled my book *Truth and Method*. What method defines is precisely *not* truth. It in no way exhausts it.

D U T T : One would hardly do justice to the importance of the third part of *Truth and Method* if one limited oneself to the theses you develop there regarding the essential connection of understanding and linguisticality to the understanding of what has been handed down to us, to our conversation with the text of tradition. Because under the category of what you call the "ontological turn of hermeneutics following the lead of language" (*GW* 1: 385–494/*TM* 383–491) you not only thematize the connection of language and understanding to the famous *Sein zum Text* [Being toward the text], you go beyond this to present the hermeneutical function of language *in the totality of our life-praxis.* For your thesis that "the fusion of horizons which takes place in understanding is language's great accomplishment" (*GW* 1: 383/*TM* 378) applies to "all forms of living together in community"[17] (GW 1: 450/*TM* 446). What is language, that it is able to do this?

GADAMER : To this question I can only answer that I am in full agreement with Wittgenstein's famous sentence: "There is no private language." Whoever speaks a "language" that nobody else understands is not really speaking. Language is not something assigned by individual human subjects. Language is a *we*, in that we are assigned our place in relation to each other, and in which the individual has no fixed borders. This means, however, that we all must overstep our own personal borders/limits of understanding in order to understand. This is what happens in the living exchange of conversation [*Gespräch*]. All living together in community is living together in language, and language exists only in conversation.[18]

DUTT : You have taken up again and again the philosophy of conversation that you first presented in Part Three of *Truth and Method* and have developed it in further writings right up to the present time.

GADAMER : Yes, this is the essence of what I have been working on over the past thirty years.

DUTT : Perhaps one can even say that what many of your writings have in common, though they are widely scattered in terms of genre, is that they are all attempts at conversation. For instance, your essay in social philosophy which talks about the meaning of friendship in the situation of its loss,[19] and your interpretation of the poetry of Celan, which inquires into the interplay of the *I* and *Thou* of lyrical speaking,[20] and many other writings, seem to be unified in a movement of thought which is dedicated to the dialogical experience within our lives. I think one needs to emphasize this orientation in such a way that in it a counterposition to Heidegger emerges, although it is never presented as this in your writings. When you spoke at the beginning of our conversation about the interpretation of the famous line of Hölderlin to the effect that "we are a conversation"—this became clear to me again. In *Truth and Method* is there not a hidden critique of Heidegger?

Being and Time seems trapped in viewing the forms of decline found in inauthentic speaking. It is true that Heidegger's 1939 Nietzsche lectures thematized *wechselweise Verständigung* [mutual understanding] as the "primary relationship" of human beings, but these lectures immediately rejected the "widely held opinion" that "reaching an understanding is already giving in, weakness, avoiding argument," and instead proclaimed that "reaching an understanding is the highest and most difficult *struggle* [Kampf] to attain the essential goal that historical humanity erects above itself."[21] Perhaps the martial ideology of these sentences may be one of the reasons you have sought another understanding of understanding? Finally, it also strikes me that in your writings that deal with conversation you do not get into the kind of ruminations one finds in the later Heidegger. For instance, he says: "No more will I call every talking with one another a conversation"; from now on he wants to hear this word in such a way "that it names for us the gathering around the essence of language."[22] I don't find this suggestion in your writings.

G A D A M E R : True, I do not make it, but I do follow it!

D U T T : In any case, don't certain distinguishing features come into play in your quest for an understanding through dialogue which seem to take up positively the "generally accepted opinion" that Heidegger rejected, and don't you put them forward as what you want to make acceptable? For instance, in *Truth and Method* you say that "one must respond to the other person," that "partners should seek to *accept* what in the partner is foreign and opposing," and when "one lets something be said," one "does not remain what one was" (*GW* 1: 389, 390, 346, 384/*TM* 385, 387, 340, 379). I find in these citations not simply a difference in content from what we referred to in Heidegger; rather, in the divergences in what you each determine to be the case I see a difference in the *form* of your theory, in your philosophical "method."

G A D A M E R : That could be.

D U T T : I would like to put it this way: You differ from Heidegger in that you are not seeking to forge a whole new conversational and communicative consciousness but rather to make more explicit the already existing understanding of what a conversation is. For this reason, you refer to what is expressed in our everyday language by the terms *Verständigung* [reaching an understanding] and *Miteinanderreden* [talking with each other]. In a short autobiographical text, you have replied to a famous turn of phrase of Heidegger in his "Letter on Humanism" in a way that is very revealing in this connection. You say there that "language is not only the house of being [*das Haus des Seins*]; it is the house of the human being [*das Haus des Menschen*], a house where one lives, which one furnishes, and where one encounters oneself, or oneself in others . . . [this] seems to me still and always true."²³ Would it perhaps have been more Gadamerian to say the house of human *beings* rather than the house of *the* human *being* [Haus *der* Mensch statt Haus *des Menschen*]?

G A D A M E R : Nevertheless I still favor the singular! Only the individual human being has a thou [*ein Du*]. The plural sounds too collective to me. But in terms of the subject-matter I agree with you. Certainly one finds a change of perspective there. People have various gifts and talents, also. For one thing, I do not have the tremendously sharp power of thinking with which Heidegger philosophized. I have always said that one of the essential differences between Heidegger and myself lies in my carefulness in interpreting. I have interpreted more cautiously, more restrainedly, than he. For if I do not defend what is correct, then it's all over for me. Heidegger could also defend an interpretation that was incorrect.

D U T T : But that would be sophistry.

G A D A M E R : No, it was not sophistry! Heidegger had such great powers of persuasion and was very compelling in the reasons why he made the mistake. I have experienced many examples of this with him, encounters in which I said to him, "But listen, Herr Heidegger, thus and thus is how the matter really stands." And finally he would answer, "Yes, there you could be right." But then he would immediately ask: "And what does that mean? That everything in Heidegger is wrong?" "No," I would answer, "not everything. But *that* was incorrect." "Yes, you could be right on that one," he would mutter. And then, later on, he would nevertheless let what was completely incorrect be printed! Now, what this means is that Hölderlin [in this case] was not as important to him as his own thinking.

D U T T : This does not exactly display a willingness to learn, and it is surely no example of what you call understanding of how to reach an agreement together. One could better call it a case of narcissism and inquire psychoanalytically into what was behind it.

G A D A M E R : No. Why would you inquire into what was behind it psychoanalytically? What I would rather do is pose once again the questions Heidegger posed. In truth, Heidegger's excursion into poetry came because of a desperate *Sprachnot* [need for language]. Heidegger was seeking concepts for a really new way of questioning, concepts that would make a temporal structure visible as truly the basic nature of being. And to do this, he turned to poetry. To Stephan George, to Georg Trakl, to the "earth" in Hölderlin, and finally more and more to Hölderlin.

D U T T : More precisely to his *misreadings* of him.

G A D A M E R : No, no! They are often powerful misreadings. And in spite of this, Heidegger's interpretations of Hölderlin are always more fruitful than all others.

D U T T : But to come back to the contrasts found in Heidegger's writings and your own with respect to the interpretation of conversation, and of our linguistic being with one another, let me turn to one of your most important texts on this topic. In your essay, "The Incapacity for Conversation" [Die Unfähigkeit zum Gespräch, *GW* 2: 207–215], I read the following: "Although our sensory perception of the world can never be anything but private, we are nevertheless also united in our drives and interests, and our reason, which is common to all and which has the gift of grasping what is common to all, but which remains powerless against the blindness that our individuality nourishes in us. So conversation with another person, whatever the objections or agreements, whatever the understandings or misunderstandings, means a kind of expansion of our individuality and a probing of the possible commonality we have to which reason encourages us" (*GW* 2: 210). In this sense, wouldn't you say that hermeneutical philosophy thematizes conversation as our capacity for rational intersubjectivity?

G A D A M E R : Oh, please spare me that completely misleading concept of intersubjectivity, of a subjectivism doubled! In that passage you quoted I did not make any clever theoretical constructions at all: I said a conversation is something one gets caught up in, in which one gets involved. In a conversation one does not know beforehand what will come out of it, and one usually does not break it off unless forced to do so, because there is always something more you want to say. That is the measure of a real conversation. Each remark calls for another, even what is called the "last word" does this, for in reality the last word does not exist. The fact that conversations lead us to better insights, that indeed they have a transformative power, is certainly something each of us has already experienced personally. And it is foolish and naïve to believe that when one converses with somebody, one does not want to reach an understanding. But of course the understanding one reaches can consist of the fact that one is not able to find anything in common between two "standpoints." In such cases, one says it was "not a good conversation." But I don't like the idea of being typed as permanently occupying a "standpoint." My hermeneutical experience warns me against such pretension, because what happens to one in a conversation is really without an end.

2

AESTHETICS

D U T T : In 1981 you met Jacques Derrida in Paris. Nevertheless, the encounter did not result in a very productive discussion.[1] Derrida basically refused to engage in a genuine dialogue; I think one would have to see it this way. In the meantime, the discussion, short though it was, has been transcribed and published, and much commented on. A whole series of texts have speculated on what was omitted. Particularly important, I think, is the German documentation of the colloquium in Philippe Forget's *Text und Interpretation*[2] and the 1989 collection of essays in English focused on the encounter between Gadamer and Derrida, *Dialogue and Deconstruction*, with interesting commentary by various scholars.[3] In your 1981 lecture in Paris you acknowledged that the encounter with the French scene was "a genuine challenge." And your later retrospective essay, "*Destruktion* and Deconstruction," concludes with the sentence, "Whoever wants me to take deconstruction to heart and insists on difference stands at the beginning of a conversation, not at its end."[4] Where would you say your conversation with Derrida stands today?

G A D A M E R : The question is whether Derrida is capable of engag-

61

ing in a genuine conversation. It could be that the character of his thinking excludes this. Still, he has a speculative mind, and for this reason I
have sought to engage him as a real conversation partner, while ignoring
his forerunners. What I found particularly impressive about Derrida was
that unlike many others, when he sought to follow Heidegger, he really
began with Aristotle. Now certainly Michel Foucault was a man of com-
parable significance, but he did not stand in the line of being a genuine
continuation of Heidegger's thinking as Derrida does. To be sure there
are boundary lines between us, and one boundary, although it is probably
not a definitive one, is that Derrida sees both Heidegger and myself as
part of the logocentrist camp, and against this the result is that Nietzsche
was right. According to Derrida, there is no other way: You have to study
Nietzsche's *Joyful Wisdom*, you can only start with surprising transformations of false prior opinions, transformations tied to a moment in which
a light of illumination suddenly flashes, yet disappears again when one
once again looks for the same figure in the text.

The difference between Derrida and me, I think, is that I myself
would like to reach an understanding with him in which we can talk with
one another. As you know, he was here in Heidelberg not long ago, when
the debate over Heidegger's politics was reaching its high point.[5] After
all, as a Heideggerian, he too was a target. And so at that time [1988] he
sought contact and came to Heidelberg with a few close friends. By the
way, he has always been very friendly with me face to face. As a courtesy
and to promote intimacy, I agreed to confer in French. Of course, it did
not help that far too many people were present at the time and many
could not understand French. But still it was the same as before: Derrida's incapacity for dialogue was once again manifest. Dialogue is not his
strength. His strength is in the artful spinning of a yarn further and further, with unexpected new aspects and surprising reversals. It is like—

D U T T : —like Penelope's work?

G A D A M E R : Yes, that too, but in the case of Penelope's work,
there is a meditative bent, which I think he does not follow. I myself have
used a similar image of continually undoing something. In philosophy
the worst thing is when one cannot take one's own standpoint completely
apart and start again, but rather one believes that once one has settled a
certain point, one can simply start out from there. In philosophy what we

are trying by ever renewed seeking to attain in our thinking is the greatest possible closeness to what is in question. In this respect, I am happy not to have a single student who "represents" my philosophy. No, no. One only *represents* a firm. Philosophy is something one does oneself, because one is trying to *think!* And so all my followers are engaged in their own independent work, and this is quite often very interesting work.

D U T T : Might Hans-Robert Jauss,[6] with his reception-aesthetics, be an example? His research program is probably the best known undertaking in literary theory that takes *Truth and Method* as its starting point.

G A D A M E R : Possibly. Still, I would say that Jauss never really ventured very far into the philosophical dimension. Yes, he made some of my results presented in *Truth and Method* fruitful, for which of course I am not claiming any laurels for myself. The fact that works have a history of their reception is something we have known basically since Herman Grimm's *Raphael* [1872].[7] And it is to this lineage that Jauss belongs.

D U T T : But he has enriched his writings with an offering in theory that resembles the Prague school—

G A D A M E R : —of structuralism, certainly. Naturally I do not wish to deny the value of the so-called reception-aesthetics, neither the historiographical results nor the methodical results, including their suggestions toward standardizing the course of investigations. But I think their relation to me falls short of the mark. Those who really read me, I think, will take an interest in other things than Jauss does. Of that I am quite sure. And to tell the truth this has been so for a long time.

D U T T : On one point Jauss has attributed to his own reception-aesthetics not just the role of continuing and applying your thought but the claim to offer a corrective. I am thinking of your discussion of "The Example of the Classical" (*GW* 1: 290–295/*TM* 285–290).

G A D A M E R : Yes, and precisely there Jauss has completely misunderstood me!

D U T T : He and some of his followers see in this chapter of *Truth and Method* a form of classicism at work, a kind of classicism which recognizes only those artistic creations as worthy of understanding which, as Rainer Warning puts it, "take as their measure the prototypical uniqueness of classical antiquity."[8] This would be a classicism in which a substantialistic conception of tradition is expressed, which is certainly incompatible with the historically enlightened theoretical sections of your book. Jauss asserts that with regard to "the concept taken over from Hegel, of the classical that interprets itself"[9] you are misleading people about the truth to be found in all art and literature, even the historicity of so-called classical works, that is, about the relationship of tension between the work and the present. And according to him, you, as it were, hypostasize a transhistorical power belonging to the tradition. What Jauss calls "emanation" would be what he sees as your wrong conceptual image.[10]

G A D A M E R : Oh, oh, quite the opposite! What you are saying does not apply *at any point* to that chapter in *Truth and Method!* "The classical," as I present it, is a historical, that is, a *temporal* concept; it describes a relationship that does not designate a quality but rather a hermeneutical relation: I have called this *der Vorzug der Bewahrung* [the advantage of preserving (the past)].[11] This does not have the remotest connection either with the Neoplatonic doctrine of emanation or with the stylistic ideal of classicism. But to recognize this one must avoid reading the chapter on the level of quibbles over method.

D U T T : Your critics object above all to that sentence where you do in fact quote approvingly the famous Hegelian formula: "Classical is what preserves itself, because it signifies itself and clarifies itself. . . . Something is said to each present moment as if it were specifically said to it."[12] Now Jauss cites this sentence in an abbreviated form and his abbreviating is not in order to prevent some redundance but rather has to do with the explanatory kernal of the sentence. The sentence without the omissions reads: "The classical is something that is preserved *because* it signifies itself and interprets itself; what is telling in this case is that it is not a statement about something that is missing, a mere testimony to something yet to be interpreted, but rather *it says something to a present time in each case, as if it were specifically addressed to it*" (*GW* 1: 295 f.). When one reads it unabridged, it sounds completely plausible, and in any case does not invoke traditional metaphysics. The sentence I just quoted is accessible without any special expenditure of faith or its negation. What you are really referring to, here, I think, is the semantic autonomy of the work; which means it does not require reconstruction and is not linked to a knowledge of its first historical context.[13] This is a semantic potential that is actualized *across contexts*, is transcontextual. It is self-evident that this actualization, which takes place under changing effective-historical conditions, does not always have the same meaning, but rather takes place in the consciousness of that transcontextuality in which alone the "timelessness" of the classic exists, which you designate as to this extent "a way of historical being" (*GW* 1: 295). So I agree that your explanation of the concept of the classical is not at all weighted down with metaphysics.

G A D A M E R : Yes, indeed! Here, as elsewhere, I take rather as my starting point the living meaning that resides in *language as it is used*. So when we say in ordinary language, *Das ist klassisch*—That is classic!— what this means is that one will hear it again and again, see it again and again, read it again and again, and it will be right again and again! That is our customary usage of language, not an artificially constructed definition. In this respect, my concept of the classical is far removed from the criticisms that have been made of it. And by the way, I have never denied that we are conscious of the historical distance between us and such "classical" works, or that this distance poses problems in terms of historical knowledge of them. Without any doubt this holds true for our historically developed consciousness, for the historical attunement we self-evidently have today in confronting artistic creations. For instance, we know that Beethoven's Ninth Symphony arose in a certain context in musical history and intellectual history and is only to be understood *historically* in this context. And yet what the Ninth Symphony signifies for our understanding is far more than a system of tasks in historical reconstruction. As you have quite correctly just quoted, the work is not first a testimony to something else that we have first to interpret; rather, the work itself addresses us just as if we were its first hearers. We hear Beethoven's music, and in the hearing there is a true participation, which I expressed in *Truth and Method* with the concept of *Zugehörigkeit* [belonging]. Quite naturally this hearing preserves the artwork in ever new ways. For the sake of greater intelligibility, I am of course glad to add this.

D U T T : How do what is classic [*Klassizität*, classicity] and modernity [*Modernität*] relate to each other? I ask this not with your chapter on the classical in *Truth and Method* in mind but rather recalling your later short book, *The Relevance of the Beautiful* (*AS* 1–76/*RB* 3–53). There you criticize two forms of one-sidedness in our relation to art: the deceptive "appearance of being historical" [*historischen Schein*] on the one hand, and the deceptive "appearance of being progressive" [*progressiven Schein*] on the other.

GADAMER: Basically both of these follow the same wrong path, but in opposite directions: One undervalues the old, while the other looks down on the new and the latest thing as aberrations. In either case, one actually also spoils the view of what one believes one is favoring. In reality, we can have the one only with the other: It is within the horizon of our experiences with the modern that the great art of the past becomes the challenging topic, and vice-versa. Here—as everywhere—one must see things together. This holds above all in the case of theoretical understanding. If one wants to be fair to the situation of art in the present, one must not stop at merely describing productions by your contemporaries; rather, one must posit the contemporaneity [*Gleichzeitigkeit*, or simultaneity, which Gadamer prefers] of the old with the new, a contemporaneity which is everywhere around us, and which most certainly had an effect on the production of the new long before the rise of the postmodern. Here, difficult tasks in thinking still await us.

DUTT: With this view of contemporaneity [*Gleichzeitigkeit*], how would you describe the relationship of classicity and modernity?

GADAMER: That is quite simple: The modern that becomes obsolete does not become classic. That's the answer.

DUTT: I would like once again to come back to Derrida. You have spoken about your encounters with him in Paris and Heidelberg and about Derrida's reluctance to engage in dialogue. But what interests me above all are the topics with which Derrida's deconstruction and your hermeneutics are both dealing. One topic that has a prominent place both in Derrida and also in your own thought is the relationship between language and meaning, between word and sense. In preparation for our conversation I reread Part Three of *Truth and Method* rather carefully. There I read about the "dialectic of the word" (1: 462) and the "speculative structure of language" (1: 478). I read there that "the finite possibilities of the word are related to the intended meaning like a pointing into the infinite" (1: 473); that, on the basis of "the living virtuality of speaking" contained in each word, "an inner dimension of multiplication" breaks out (462); and that language is not the representation [*Mimesis*] of a set of pregiven meanings but is a "coming to language" from a constant reserve into an event in which meaning "announces itself." All this does not seem to me to be worlds away from what [Rodolphe] Gasché described as the "infrastructures" that Derrida brought to light in the first part of *On Grammatology* for the purpose of deconstructing the transcendental signifieds of logocentric metaphysics.[14]

Furthermore, you say in your essay "Language and Understanding" that "there is no first word."[15] Rather, "there is always already *a system of words* that is the basis of the meaning of each word" (*GW* 2: 196). In this important but far too little noticed essay you show that this "system of words" must not be mistaken for the abstract semantic concept of stable contexts. Rather, it is the always preliminary movement that is contained in speaking and further speaking: "The only thing that constitutes language," you say, "is that one word leads to another; each word is, so to speak, summoned, and on its side holds open the further progress of the speaking" (*GW* 2: 197).

Now in my view, this definitely runs parallel to the place in Derrida's fine recollection of Curtius, where he refers disparagingly to the logocentric "idea of a Book" that comprises "the already constituted totality of signifieds."[16] Have you yourself not also gone beyond this supposed totality with your idea of the play of the texts? Have you not in your own way also transgressed it in your description of the play of conversation? In other words, what I am asking is: do you not see some overlaps between certain strands of Derrida's theory and your own?

G A D A M E R : I have difficulty with this question, since I do not find that either Derrida or I can be well described using the concept of theory. And the later Derrida not at all!

D U T T : He drops theory altogether. That's what Rorty said.[17]

G A D A M E R : And there Rorty is correct. Derrida moves around *within* deconstruction.

But even so, if I accept your question with these reservations, I can at least say it seems clear to me that Derrida brought his views to a fairly definitive articulation already in *Voice and Phenomenon*.[18] Well, back in 1924 we in Germany already had similar ideas. I still remember vividly how

Karl Löwith and I were reading Husserl's *Logical Investigations* very carefully together at that time, and we came up with the same criticism that Derrida found forty years later! At that time we had Wilhelm von Humboldt in mind, while Derrida's critique was inspired by Charles Peirce. So, yes, certainly I think *Voice and Phenomenon* and *Of Grammatology* contain a great deal that is a very positive contribution to philosophy. But this is nevertheless only *the starting point* for a dialogue, as I said in the closing sentence of my essay "*Destruktion* and Deconstruction," which you have quoted. But what we are dealing with here is a conversation in which, unfortunately, Derrida is not allowing himself to get involved. Why he cannot do this I do not know. I think he suspects that the readiness to reach an understanding and the will to reach an understanding, which are the presuppositions of every conversation, magically reintroduce the transcendental signified into the event of posing and answering questions. I certainly don't want this. The "dialectic of the word," which you rightly started with, is based on the freedom of each partner, which I have never disputed but on the contrary have particularly emphasized. Conversation is the game of language, and readiness for conversation is only the entrance door into this game, not an absurd effort to hold the game within boundaries.

D U T T : May I take up one of the questions that Derrida formulated in Paris? He asked you back then what an "enlargement of context" would be. "Would it," he asked, "be a continuous expansion or a discontinuous restructuring?"[19]

G A D A M E R : To this I can only answer that I myself never know. Can I know this? Isn't the next word of my partner something I can't anticipate or control?

D U T T : What about the complaint that *Truth and Method* is one of the last great formulations of logocentric discourse? Does this apply?

G A D A M E R : I would ask those who raise this objection to please undertake a serious reading of my book. After that I would seek to begin a conversation with them. No, I believe I have learned from Heidegger that philosophy does not happen in the form of propositions and judgments. For this reason I would characterize the general direction of my own efforts as follows: Do not think against language but with language.[20]

D U T T : In the middle of your essay titled "Text and Interpretation," from your 1981 encounter with Derrida in Paris, one finds a theory with regard to the reading of literary, or as you prefer to call them, "eminent," texts.[21] If one wants to get acquainted with a major aspect of your thinking in the area of aesthetics in its most fully unfolded form, then I would say working with this text is essential. You assert in a more recent essay, "The End of Art?" that "nowhere more than in linguistic art is the cooperation of the receiver so obviously demanded. Indeed, reading is the authentic and representative form of relation to art; it is where the participation of the receiver of an artwork can most readily be grasped."[22] In keeping with this basic insight, you develop in "Text and Interpretation" a theory of reading as a theory of aesthetic understanding. This theory describes the distinctive features of the process of understanding that takes place in the encounter with works of art—both linguistic and nonlinguistic. Perhaps we could put some of the elements of this description in context.

We need first to recall the most important steps in theory that you took as you moved toward the formulation in philosophical aesthetics that you present in "Text and Interpretation." As I recall, the ontology of the work of art projected in the first part of *Truth and Method* was understood by you as a corrective to the formalistic implications of an aesthetics based on heightened experience [*Erlebnisästhetik*], which you accuse of having an inadequate concept of aesthetic experience in its hermeneutic dimension. Indeed, the summary of your analyses there puts forward a very pointed programmatic formulation: "*Aesthetics must be swallowed up in hermeneutics*" (*GW* 1: 170). Can you explain what this claim is all about?

G A D A M E R : First of all, when one speaks of "aesthetic experience" per se, one ordinarily assumes that this dimension is not concerned with the content of a work; rather, it is concerned with its form—only with the formal quality possessed by a work of art. Formalism in aesthetics feeds on this view, which, when it is not dialectically reshaped by an aesthetic of content, as it is in Hegel, dominates the discussion in a wide variety of ways. Related to this point is the sentence you cited [about aesthetics needing to be absorbed into hermeneutics], where I am also not calling for an aesthetics of content after the Hegelian model. Rather, I maintain that a work of art, thanks to its formal aspect, *has something to say to us* [italics added] either through the question it awakens, or the question it answers. A work of art "says something to someone." This is not merely a manner of speaking; this formulation occurs for a very good reason again and again in my writings, which start from the encounter with artwork. This saying points very precisely to the reality of one's concrete experience of art, a reality which got swallowed up in the abstractions of the *Erlebnisästhetik* [an aesthetics based on *Erlebnis*, heightened lived experience]. An artwork "says something to someone." In this assertion is contained the dismay of finding oneself directly affected by what was said by the work, and being forced to reflect again and again on what was said there, in order to make it understandable to oneself and to others. I therefore continue to maintain that the experience of art is an experience of meaning, and as such this experience is something that is brought about by understanding. To this extent, then, aesthetics is absorbed into hermeneutics.

D U T T : It is clearly discernible in your answer that your emphasis on the understanding character of aesthetic experience as your aesthetic approach is not supposed to lead to a new version of idealistic aesthetics. True, in *Truth and Method* you admire Hegel's lectures in aesthetics because they bring about a recognition of the orientation to meaning "that is to be found in all experience of art and that at the same time is mediated by the historical consciousness" (*GW* 1: 103/*TM* 98). On the other hand, you do not embrace the systematic character of Hegel's idealism, which for Hegel resulted in the semantic offer of a world history of art, grasped conceptually, that he designed and constructed with great attention to detail, and that he wanted to pass on to future generations. Rather, for you the experience of art cannot be overbid or surpassed by theory any more than the traditions of religion and history can. In your little book, *The Relevance of the Beautiful*, published in 1977, this point turns into a fundamental critique based specifically on the aesthetic experience. Taking up certain terms from Heidegger's essay on the artwork,[23] you show that idealistic aesthetics fails to grasp the special character of the experience of art because German Idealism describes this experience as a "pure integration of meaning."[24] What idealistic aesthetics overlooks, you assert, is the "resistance" of the aesthetic object, which you call the "resistance of the work."[25]

G A D A M E R : Yes, indeed. At that time I explained this by pointing to Hegel's famous definition of the beautiful as "the sensuous appearing of the idea." Obviously what is presupposed in this definition is that one is able to go beyond the specific type of appearance, the specific manner of sensory representation. It assumes that the philosophical thought which thinks the idea constitutes the highest and most appropriate form of truth. If one describes aesthetic thinking according to this model, this means that the first powerful impact [*Betroffenheit*] produced by a work of art, about which I just spoke, the first indeterminate expectation of meaning through which the work of art becomes meaningful, could find a fixed semantic fulfillment such that the whole of its meaning would have been understood once and for all and thus "brought into our possession," so to speak. Were this the case, the work of art would be just a "carrier of meaning" like a letter or a newspaper story, which we lay aside after we have understood the news it brings and have gotten the end-meaning. But our understanding of artwork is manifestly not of this type. Everyone knows this from his or her own encounters with art, from concerts, visits to museums, and from her or his reading.

One does not possess the meaning of a work of art in the kind of way that would allow one to speak of a transfer of meaning. The meaning of a work of art can never be simply transferred. A work of art must itself be *there* [*muß da sein*]. You can find substitute forms for a carrier of meaning. You can tell a friend over the telephone what the the content of a letter was, and you can paraphrase a newspaper story. You cannot paraphrase a poem. You cannot substitute something else for it. But you can memorize it, so that it is *there* when you say it, and is *there* again and again. By the way, the term "aesthetic object" seems to me a completely unsuitable concept. When a work of art truly takes hold of us, it is not an object that stands opposite us which we look at in hope of seeing through it to an intended conceptual meaning. Just the reverse. The work is an *Ereignis*—an *event* that "appropriates us" into itself. It jolts us, it knocks us over, and sets up a world of its own, into which we are drawn, as it were. Heidegger has persuasively described this *Ereignis*-character of the artwork in his essay on the origin of a work of art.[26] He recognized the tension that characterizes a work of art when it "sets up a world" and at the same time sets this world into a resting form and fixes it there. This is a double motion, in which the work resists the claim to a pure integration of sense that believes itself to be superior. Heidegger calls this the struggle between world and earth in the work of art, and in my opinion, in doing so he overcame the idealist interpretation of art. It is in the sheer being there [*Dasein*] of the work of art that our understanding experiences the depths and unfathomability of its meaning.

D U T T : In this connection, you yourself have made the suggestion that the word *Gebilde* [a structure or construct] should be used in place of the word "work" in reference to works of art.

G A D A M E R : Yes, precisely in order to showcase the fact that a *Gebilde* molds itself as if taking its own unified form from within, and it is *there*. It is not, for instance, like some kind of construction for which there would be a blueprint. No, a *Gebilde* is precisely not "constructed" in this sense. What this entails is that all *our* constructions, all our efforts to understand *Gebilde* through constructions, *must each time be taken back*. We must come back again and again to the *Gebilde* itself, beginning each time anew.

For instance, take the example of this Poliakoff, which has hung in its place now [in Gadamer's tiny study] for thirty years. My students gave it to me on the occasion of my sixtieth birthday. Again and again as I sit where you are now sitting, I begin to reflect and I ask myself: What do I really see there? I look at it, but I do not write an interpretation. So, what do I see? What does it really say? *Je ne sais quoi.*[27] On the left I see a black cross, a half cross, and it holds my eye. Farther to the left there is a red area on the left near the frame which seems to form a figure almost like a face. This could be a head in profile. Perhaps. So the picture constantly speaks with me. I look at it again and again. It compels me to come back [*zurückzukommen*] to it over and over.

D U T T : Perhaps I can take this as my cue to ask you once again about "Text and Interpretation." In this text, you used the term *Zurückkommen* [coming back] as the mark of the literary or "eminent" text; indeed, you have made this part of your definition of such texts. You point out that other kinds of texts, like those we meet in everyday experience, "are just a phase in the process of understanding," but linguistic works of art "stand in themselves" (*GW* 2: 357/*DD* 47). They "are only truly there in our *coming back* to them," you say, and this experience always awaits us

Serge Poliakoff, *Composition, Twentieth Century,* Lithograph
(57.6 × 43.4 cm). Achenbach Foundation for Graphic Arts

also in the case of reading in the strongest sense of the word (*GW* 2: 351/ *DD* 41–42). For the act of reading this obviously means more than an increase in our difficulty in understanding [and we must therefore come back to the text]; certainly one can also run into difficulty in understanding in the case of other texts, for example scientific prose. What it means, if I have understood it correctly, is that in the encounter with literary texts the reading itself undergoes a change.

GADAMER: Well, I would first like to say this: *Lesen ist Verstehen* [To read is to understand]. Reading *is* understanding.[28] Whoever does not understand is not reading; he or she is only sounding out letters and saying words. In cases of oral reading one notices this, when the reader has failed in the task of really catching the meaning. When one listens to such a reader one can then scarcely understand anything. Of course, this is an exceptional case. As a rule, a reader understands the text at least well enough that he or she is basically directed toward what the text says. One can also observe this when one is trying to remove difficulties in understanding. One looks up the word one does not know in the dictionary and then proceeds. Thus far, the text is in fact only a carrier of meanings, as I have called it earlier. A text that is only a transporter of meanings will disappear as soon as its meaning is delivered, but literary texts do not disappear after they are read. All speaking, which naturally applies to literary texts as well, has a meaning that one tries to understand. In literary texts, the words carry in themselves the meaning of the speaking, a meaning which the reader, with a pragmatic attitude, is seeking to know. But words in being merely passed on do not really open up. The words of a literary work, however, properly read, become present in themselves, present through an exactly right sound, in the reality of their sounds, and in a fullness of meaning whose play extends beyond the limits erected by the context of their speaking.

In what we call literature a special kind of counterplay is characteristic—naturally in various shadings of meaning—a counterplay between the intended meaning and the self-presentation of the language. We don't find this elsewhere, and of course this has consequences for our reading of it. I have tried to show that the relationship between text and interpretation is changed from the ground up when one is dealing with literary texts. This is why I speak of them as *eminent* texts. By an "eminent" text I mean something very precise, namely that through the weaving together of its individual strands such a text has nothing that can be separated from it; thus it is truly a *text,* a text in the eminent sense. Any pulling out of the threads of meaning that happens in an interpretation demands that they also be re-interwoven once more. What such coming-back-to-the-text-once-again[29] in reality means is letting the text speak.

D U T T : But if I have correctly followed your line of argument in the essay we are discussing ["Text and Interpretation"], your point is that this coming back or this having-to-go-back—at one point you said that one will even be *"thrown* back" (*GW* 2: 358/*DD* 48)—itself constitutes the content of the experience of reading, and this experience is not something that comes in a subsequent observation that one makes in a later reading, or also possibly does not make.

G A D A M E R : I have in fact a short while ago alluded to the tension between construction and *Gebilde* [structure]. One knows the word *Konstruktion* [construction] or *konstruieren* [to construe] from having had instruction in ancient languages. There the student must "construe" the sentence in order to understand the meaning of the parts of the sentence. Then when the sentence is rightly construed, understanding often happens like a blow. The hermeneutical movement toward [the meaning of] a text—that is to say, reading—can be compared step for step to this. One first construes the part that one is perceiving on the basis of a unitary sense of the whole. One follows an expectation of meaning to which one holds fast, up to the moment the whole comes together. One must then, of course, always correct this if the text demands it. There can be no doubt that this basic structure of hermeneutic motion, present in every reading of something, is also in play in the case of literary texts. Here, too, understanding moves toward the unity of the *Gebilde.*

At the same time, with a literary text it is not the case that we hurriedly follow the line of meaning just so we can reach the end-meaning. Rather, we pause again and again, we come back and discover each time new relationships of meaning and sound which the self-presencing of language opens up to us. And we do not just pause; we turn the natural direction of the movement in reading around one hundred eighty degrees, so to speak. We page back, we "get into" the reading and move ever deeper into the world of the art-structure [*des Gebildes*]. In fact, one can even say we are "thrown back" into it, not because we have reached an impasse but because this world of meaning and sound is of such inexhaustible fullness that it will not let go of us.

D U T T : In "Text and Interpretation" you speak of the "volume" of a literary text (*GW* 2: 353/*DD* 44).

G A D A M E R : Yes, it is precisely this that constitutes the volume of a text: the fullness of changing realities of sound and relationships of meaning which does not disappear into the mere teleology of seeking a meaning.

D U T T : If one would like to take this term "volume" seriously as referring not just to a kind of decoration or accompanying background but rather as a dimension of the experience of understanding a work of art, then must one not come to the conclusion that the hermeneutical identity that a meaning-oriented sort of reading develops by following the line of sense in a text becomes in the case of literary texts a broken identity? Isn't what you call "volume" a hermeneutical identity that constantly pushes beyond the boundaries of the self-sameness of its meaning? Is it not the shattering of boundaries that one experiences in the process of reading [a great work]?

G A D A M E R : That could well be, but is the reading of such texts really only a reading? Is this reading not also a singing? Is the process by which a poem comes to speak a process that is carried out only by the intended meaning? Or is there not at the same time in the poem a kind of *Vollzugswahrheit* [a truth that emerges through the performance]? To carry out this performance is the task that the poem imposes. Is this not what the picture that is not merely a copy imposes? In the two culminating essays of volume 8 (*Kunst als Aussage* [Art as Assertion]) of my *Gesammelte Werke*, which appeared this year [1993], I have tried to work out what this *Vollzugswahrheit* means.[30]

D U T T : You characterize the encounter with a work of art, which is experienced as an unfathomable structure [*Gebilde*], as a tarrying [*Verweilen*]. This tarrying, you say, is the temporal form of the experience of art.

G A D A M E R : The temporal dimension that is bound up with art is, in fact, fundamental. In this tarrying the contrast with the merely pragmatic realms of understanding becomes clear. The *Weile* [the "while" in

Verweilen, tarrying] has this very special temporal structure—a temporal structure of being moved, which one nevertheless cannot describe merely as duration, because duration means only further movement in a single direction. This is not what is determinative in the experience of art. In it we tarry, we remain with the art structure [*Kunstgebilde*], which as a whole then becomes ever richer and more diverse. The *volume* increases infinitely—and for this reason we learn from the work of art how to tarry.

D U T T : The terrorism of the "culture industry" has reached new heights in the last decade [1983–1993]. With video technology and the licensing of so-called private television, the intensive bombardment of consumers with advertising has become more and more possible. The explosion of attractions goes on unpunctuated by the earlier long spaces of time between commercials. However much energy one expends in discourse that tries to put a postmodern legitimation on what is going on there, one thing is clear: tarrying has found no place in this medium. In your commemorative talk on Heidegger, you spoke of "an aesthetic culture that is withering away."[31] Would you say that tarrying is now disappearing?

G A D A M E R : That is a possibility, but probably not. In any case, one must not give up! I believe that the creative minds of our society are steering clear of this, or else will manage to free themselves of it in the future. In the end, I think, people will not be able to endure for long doing exactly what everyone else is doing in their so-called free time. So no, I believe tarrying is something that will always exist. Otherwise the new, as it sweeps along, will become far too boring.

3'

PRACTICAL

PHILOSOPHY

D U T T : In your more recent writings from the seventies and eighties, you lay special stress on the link between hermeneutics and practical philosophy. In *Truth and Method* the basis for your conception of practical philosophy is established through an interpretation of Aristotle's *Ethics*. Could you explain what practical philosophy means in the tradition of Aristotle and what structural affinity exists between it and hermeneutics?

G A D A M E R : First of all, one needs to be aware that the word "praxis" should not be understood in too narrow a sense—for instance in the sense that one makes "practical applications" of scientific theories. Certainly the familiar contrast between theory and practice brings these two terms into proximity with each other, and the application of theories surely belongs in our practice. But this is not all there is to the meaning of "praxis." It means much more than the obvious relation to theory suggests. The word "praxis" points to the totality of our practical life, all our human action and behavior, the self-adaptation of the human being as a whole in this world. Thus it has to do also with one's politics, political advising and consulting, and our passing of laws. Our praxis, in short, is our "form of life." And this is the topic of the practical philosophy which Aristotle established.

The Greek polis, including the praxis of its free citizens, stood before the gaze of Aristotle. Aristotle showed how, in contrast to the orders of life to which animals belong, the orders of human living together in a polis were not predetermined, were not instinctually assured. And yet this living together took place in an orderly way, when it was led by reason. This rationality that guides practice Aristotle calls *phronesis* [practical wisdom]. *Phronesis* is something that proves itself only in the concrete situation and stands always already within a living network of common convictions, habits, and values—that is to say, within an *ethos*.

This is where the hermeneutical problem, whose relation to practical philosophy you asked about, comes in. Determining what is rational in the specific, concrete situation in which you find yourself—which certainly can have many parallels to other situations yet remains the specific situation in which you stand—is something you must do for yourself. What is rational in the sense of the right thing to do in this situation is not prescribed to you in the general orientations you have been given about good and evil in the same way that the instructions for use that come with a tool tell you how to use it. Rather, you have to determine for yourself what you are going to do. And to do this you have to arrive at a comprehension of your situation, reach an understanding with yourself about it. In other words, you have to *interpret* it! That, then, is the hermeneutical dimension of ethics and of practical reason. Hermeneutics is *die Kunst der Verständigung*—the art of reaching an understanding —of something or with someone. I think you can see immediately that this "coming to an understanding" of our practical situations and what we must do in them is not monological; rather, it has the character of a conversation. We are dealing with each other. Our human form of life has an "I and thou" character and an "I and we" character, and also a "we and we" character. In our practical affairs we depend on our ability to arrive at an understanding. And reaching an understanding happens in conversation, in a dialogue.

D U T T : But of course Aristotle in his ethics could presuppose a stable structure of norms, which circumscribed the space of understanding and behavior. With us it is different.

G A D A M E R : With us, too, there have been times of more or less authoritarian education full of self-evident customs, which one was not allowed to transgress under any circumstances. We have largely shaken these off today, and I find this very pleasing in many ways. One is not bossed around as much. But life has become more difficult. In this respect, Arnold Gehlen with his neoconservativism was right in asserting that institutions actually take a load off of us and our society.

D U T T : Yes, Gehlen was nostalgic about institutions. He wanted to regress, to go back. Away with discussion and back to obedience.

G A D A M E R : But that is absolutely impossible! And this is the reason I have directed my thinking toward formulating a philosophy of rational self-responsibility and toward showing the communicative character of our praxis. We must find the paths ourselves: the paths of solidarity and of reaching understandings. Among the tasks of politics today, I think a top priority should be to make us more generally aware of our deep solidarities.

D U T T : In the past few months a number of terrible things have happened here in Germany. When one looks at the neo-Nazi perpetrators of violence and at the people who are clapping in applause, one gets worried that human solidarity among us Germans is only a crumbling façade, that indeed the opposite seems to be coming back again. The solidarity expressed by the government does not reach the victims of the racists anymore. How can we in Germany find a real solidarity with those who come to us in deep need and distress? I ask this, by the way, fresh from reading your very recent comments in the magazine *Sinn und Form* [*Meaning and Form*] on the political incompetence of philosophy. There you express yourself very skeptically about questions of this type. The example you give is Jean Beaufret's question about ethics posed to Heidegger. You say there: "There is no conciliatory ethics."[1]

G A D A M E R : Well, I really think we are becoming ever more aware of the solidarities that now exist. Think of the many human beings who are taking to the streets, to make chains of lights, to demonstrate, and to attend conferences! These are encouraging efforts to shape public opinion and to give our solidarities an appropriate presence in the media. We do not have to invent these solidarities; we merely have to make ourselves aware of them.

I am persuaded that this holds true for the whole problem of ethics. Aristotle was quite simply right when he said that whoever has not been trained into a real *ethos*—either by himself or by others—cannot grasp what ethics is. What we are dealing with here is not some special task of philosophy. We are dealing here with a responsibility we all carry! What my little piece in *Sinn und Form* intends to say is this: It is never only the other side who is guilty. Take the problem of atomic energy, for example. Fundamentally, the protest movement against atomic energy is expressing a genuine solidarity. True, it has been exploited in seemingly absurd ways from very different sides; and naturally, one can say in advance that the water management people and the coal industry will be against atomic energy. But such efforts by special interests to take possession of this spontaneous movement and lead it into detours still cannot call into question the basic human solidarity that this and other movements reflect.

By the way, I am convinced that our thinking today within the framework not only of the nation-state but also of Europe is proving to be outdated. Isolation from the rest of the world is no longer possible. Humanity today is sitting in a rowboat, as it were, and we must steer this boat in such a way that we do not all crash into the rocks. This conviction will grow constantly. Of course this does not mean that we won't still feel traces of the winds of nationalism. But the worldwide interwovenness of economies can perhaps have a preventive function. Whether business acts with honor or dishonor, one thing is certain: only through economic help can the stream of immigration [into Germany] from the poorer countries come to a stop. Anything else is not only not showing solidarity but is destined to have little success. As long as shortages reign in Poland, Rumania, Bulgaria, or wherever, and the living conditions are so bad that people do not want to stay there, they will continue to come here. Of course we must not stop with such basic matters. These alone will not reestablish solidarity. Solidarities are experienced in all those things where, when many people have a share in them, they do not lose their value but on the contrary their value increases[2]—which is also the case with what we call art and culture.

D U T T : In Schopenhauer's philosophy, solidarity is all-encompassing. It is not understood as merely a relation between human beings, for the same will to live is present in all living things. The *principium individuationis*, the nonidentity with the all, is just an illusion. It is true that we cling to this illusion—and to the illusion that animals and nature are material for our use.

GADAMER: Indeed, I do not find myself very far from these Schopenhauerian thoughts. The laws for the protection of animals, nature, and also children, are, I believe, examples where we find expressions of true solidarity; indeed, we have institutionalized many of our solidarities. Think of the corresponding laws, and the associations that are seeking to foster such a consciousness.

DUTT: If I understand correctly, for you the establishing of institutions is not the most important thing, but rather the public discussion of these questions. The "disburdening-effect" of having all these institutions results in an unconcerned attitude that assumes that the institutions must already be taking care of things. On the other hand, the need to support the unions against the lobbies of profit-seekers is obvious. So don't you think we must try above all to carry forward the public discussion?

GADAMER: Yes, but one must do more than advance the public discussion. One must also do something oneself; and indeed one is already doing something [right or wrong]. Praxis, however, means to act, and that starts with an alert consciousness. Conscious action is more than just doing something. A human being is one who controls *himself or herself.* This involves self-control, self-testing, and setting an example. For this reason, *ethos* is not without *logos*, as I have shown with regard to Aristotle.

DUTT: Your works arguing for the contemporary relevance of practical philosophy are directed against normativistic moral philosophy—

GADAMER: —against an ethics of the *ought*, that overlooks the hermeneutical problem that only when one makes concrete and individual what people hold in common does it acquire its particular content.

DUTT: Nevertheless, you do, above all, turn against an instrumentalistically abbreviated concept of rationality, against the objective and subjective forms of what you call "the degeneration of practice [*Praxis*] into technology."[3] Here your philosophy does become a critique of society.

GADAMER: But you can find the critique of instrumental reason already in the Frankfurt School.[4]

D U T T : Exactly. I myself wanted to point out this area of agreement you have with the Frankfurt School.

G A D A M E R : I have always seen myself in agreement with it on a whole series of points. As you know, I wanted to begin a dialogue with Adorno, but his death [in 1969] intervened.

D U T T : Of course one does not find in your thought the pessimism that predominates in the late texts of Adorno and Horkheimer. The gesture of your texts is different from this. You are more confident.

G A D A M E R : Yes, I am very skeptical of every kind of pessimism. I find in all pessimism a certain lack of sincerity.

D U T T : Why?

G A D A M E R : Because no one can live without hope.

D U T T : But to express hope, of course, does not mean that you join the chorus of philosophers of cheer.

G A D A M E R : Most certainly not! Naturally one cannot keep quiet about the negative.

D U T T : You have warned very strongly against the undermining of reason in society through the false ideals held by a society full of experts and functionaries.

G A D A M E R : Oh, yes, here lies a danger which we really have to keep continually in mind, and which we must energetically work against! Of course, in the highly technologized industrialized society in which we live the expert is a phenomenon that we certainly would not wish away. Experts have become indispensable in the most varied realms, in order to assure the requisite management and control of complex theoretical and technical processes. But it is an error to think that "the experts"—the business and economic experts, the environmental experts, or the military experts—can take away from us our praxis in society and relieve us from decisions on matters we all have to deal with as political citizens working with each other, matters that we all have to face and deal with. And certainly in our modern society, based as it is on the division of labor, we are all functionaries in the sense that in our various occupations we carry out highly specialized functions. This specialization and arrangement in a fixed structure of tasks is, nevertheless, not the whole of a societal existence. It does not really contain the truth about our form of life. In reality, our praxis does not consist in our adapting to pregiven functions or in the thinking out of suitable means for achieving pregiven purposes. That is technology. Rather, our praxis must consist in prudent choices as we pursue common common goals, choices we arrive at together and in practical reflection making concrete decisions about what is to be done in our present situation. That is societal reason [*gesellschaftliche Vernunft*]!

D U T T : Your diagnosis of our time brings your critique of negative developments together with a look at the resources of social reason, resources that have developed historically. You refer us to a semantics of humanity and maturity that is anchored in the ancient community cherishing the Christian tradition. And you mention the forms of discourse found in the critique of ideology and utopian thinking. The neo-conservatives announce the end of socialistic utopian thinking. With the collapse of socialistic dictatorships in the east such thinking is said to be no longer in favor. Must one accept this view, or may one hold fast to your writings from the seventies, according to which for our praxis utopia remains an indispensable "suggestiveness from afar"?[5]

G A D A M E R : Yes I certainly do believe this, and I believe it will continue to be valid in the future. By the way, I did not come up with this phrase about "the suggestiveness from afar" during a time of freedom but during the Third Reich! Perhaps you know my recent critique of Popper in "Plato's Thought in Utopia"?[6] In this I try to show that it is totally impossible to talk appropriately about Plato if one does not understand how to talk appropriately about utopias. The *Republic* and the *Laws* are utopias, and as I point out in that essay, utopias are a Greek genre of literature. One other thing is fully clear: Where no freedom of speech prevails, one can only practice critique in such indirect forms. Indeed, this is precisely its primary function: critique of the present, not the construction of whatever project being described in the work. The *Republic* is a classical example of a critique of nepotism. For certainly one cannot take seriously the idea that Plato thinks children ought to be brought up away from their parents. But he did in fact mean that one's degree of relationship to the powerful should not to be determinative for the distribution of power![7]

D U T T : In "What is Praxis?" you also give "instructions for reflection" for social reason.[8]

GADAMER: Yes, indeed! Utopias are texts that will really cause us to think, and to reflect on our relationships, if only we understand how to read them. They do not deal with an appeal to do this or that here and now. Not at all. Ernst Bloch has represented this point very effectively in his way.[9] The utopias that he lectured about had an imaginative power about them that truly stimulated reflection. Of course, like all the rest of us scholars, his intellect was not genuinely political.

DUTT: He did work to prevent politics from degenerating into the administration of what is.

GADAMER: I agree. One ought never to allow dogmatism to stifle utopian fantasy and readiness for reflection, even when dogmatism gives itself an appearance of analytical sobriety. That is really very far from what I mean. What I also mean is that we can only protect and further develop solidarities on the broad basis of opinion culture that is not consciously steered by us—certainly not by the philosophers—but comes into existence by itself.

My favorite image in this respect is Field Marshall Kutuzov in Tolstoy's *War and Peace*. Before the battle with Napoleon to defend Moscow, he slept through the final counsel of war with the generals and awoke to say, "Yes, certainly do it as you have said," and then he climbed on his horse and rode around the camp to all the night-fires and spoke with individual people. Of course, the question is, who was the real victor in this battle? Behind all this stands a theory that we all, as I believe, must accept: We are integral, only integral [*Integrale*]. None of us knows what effect he or she really has as our actions are integrated into a larger context. That does not mean that we ought not to think about these matters nor that in our thinking we should not debate with the critique of ideology, or with utopias.

PART II

THREE
OTHER
CONVERSATIONS

4

THE GREEKS,
OUR TEACHERS

with Glenn W. Most

M O S T :[1] Professor Gadamer, how did you arrive at the Greeks?

GADAMER: In a quite roundabout way! Of course, I learned Greek and Latin in grammar school and high school [*Gymnasium*], but this was during the hard times of the First World War. In those days we did not have the excellent teachers that we otherwise would have had, but, on the contrary, dreadfully bigoted and reactionary old fogeys. For instance, when in a particular reading lesson we came to the fact that the Spartan male and female students did their gymnastic exercises together naked, the teacher asked, "Is that good?" and compelled us to answer, "No, that is not good!" As a consequence of the powerful impression these experiences made on me during my youth, I steered completely clear of classical philology when I entered the University of Breslau. I was also unaffected by my decidedly natural-scientific family background and turned to all other possibilities that seemed worth learning. Above all, these were the study of languages, literature, and art, until in Marburg I took my first steps in philosophy and chose to do my doctoral work under Paul Natorp. He suggested that I read Fichte, an idea which instantly

made sense to me, for I already perceived that the so-called NeoKantian-
ism was really not this but a form of Fichteanism. But I really knew nothing else about Fichte, so the first thing I read was the exchange of letters
between Fichte and his fiancée, later his wife. Well, I went immediately
to Natorp and said, "Oh, Sir, I would really prefer to work on Plato!" At
that time I had just turned twenty and was really quite immature. So the
famous scholar and thinker Paul Natorp suggested to me the topic of
pleasure in the Platonic dialogues, and I then undertook to present a
more fundamental reading of Plato than was required by his suggested
topic. Natorp was pleased with this, but there was actually nothing of real
value in it. Mercifully, this work [his doctoral dissertation] has found its
rightful place in the mausoleum for the forgotten. After that, I gradually
turned to doing some work on Aristotle, first of all under my other
teacher, Nicolai Hartmann. I already had a basic knowledge of Plato, and
my Greek was good enough to read the text without a dictionary. I soon
reached the point where I found Aristotle very interesting, and I wanted
to pursue the topic of pleasure further, but now in Aristotle. Nicolai
Hartmann approached Aristotle in a rather shallow phenomenological
way in order gain distance from his own NeoKantian transcendental philosophy, so I set out for Freiburg, with Hartmann's blessing, in order to
study with the young assistant of Husserl, Martin Heidegger, whose unpublished studies in Aristotle had become known through transcripts
and copies. This brought a complete about-face for me. All at once I saw
how misleading the whole scholastic conceptual grid was. I saw how, by
means of this, people loved to represent Aristotelian philosophy as "real-
istic," even when they themselves were not Thomists. Of course, this
complaint could not really be applied to Nicolai Hartmann, yet somehow even he employed clichés like realism and idealism, that had become
suspect for me at that time under the influence of Dilthey. Also, Heidegger was incorporating historicality into his thinking. I learned from Heidegger, to my great astonishment, that what Aristotle meant by the term
"rational animal"—or man, the being that has reason—was that man had
language! It is in this way, then, that I first undertook to study Aristotle,
above all the *Ethics*, as a way somehow to make amends for my dissertation on Plato. I did not succeed, however, because for this task my Greek
and my knowledge of philological ways of working in general were not at

all sufficient. So in 1924 I turned to the study of classical philology—above all, as a way of counterbalancing the power of Heidegger's over-whelming philosophical impact. Because I really did not want to become simply a cheap imitation and echo of Heidegger. Rather than do that, I decided I would qualify myself to become at least a decent high school teacher. So I went to Paul Friedländer, who was at that time writing his great work on Plato, and I came to appreciate and value Friedländer's enormous feeling for language.[2] I was helped in this also by a friend, Friedrich Klingner. Friedländer's arguments were often wrong, but his aesthetic sensibility was just tremendous. The unlocking of the scenes of the Platonic dialogues, for example, I owe in large part to my interaction with Friendländer. I was able to conclude my philological studies in a rel-atively short time, while simultaneously continuing with my philosophi-cal work, and now I knew myself to be quite differently prepared in phi-losophy than I had been before my three years of training in classical philology.

After passing the state examination in classical philology [in 1927], I undertook anew to understand Plato's *Philebus* on the basis of the phe-nomenological analysis of problems. This is a very difficult dialogue. As everybody knows, it belongs to an apparently late phase of Plato's work. Here Socrates emerges once again as the conductor of the dialogue and, as I more and more realized, he already comes close in this dialogue to what later became Aristotelian practical philosophy.

It was in this way, then, that I began my serious interest in things Greek. Through the Greeks I hoped to arrive at my own independent philosophical work, namely, to recognize the dogmatic rigidness of sharply contrasting Plato and Aristotle. After I had attained through philology a living relationship with the Greek classics, then I worked my way back into philosophy. This path of mine also had the blessing of Heidegger, of course, who basically was my model, without my wishing to be his imitator. What one could learn from Heidegger, above all, was precisely this: Greek words, even if they have a conceptual function, re-main *words* and thus they draw their conceptual meaning from living lan-guage. I have learned that one can only free oneself from the large echo of the latinized Middle Ages in philosophy—an echo that has held more or less undisputed sway right into our century—if one learns what the

Greeks learned: to draw conceptual meanings from their living, spoken language.

M O S T : After the First World War and into the twenties, Greek philosophy seems to have aroused stronger and stronger interest among German philosophers. I am thinking, for instance, of the NeoKantians, of the writings of Julius Stenzel and Ernst Hoffmann, and of the rediscovery of the Presocratics. How do you explain this, and how was it for you personally to study and to work in this context?

G A D A M E R : It is of course not easy to answer this question. At the time, we were ourselves busy interrogating our own existence. We forged onward in the current of the time. If I pose the question with reference to myself, personally, certainly the "Marburg School" was of importance. Along with Hermann Cohen there was, above all, Paul Natorp, a most outstanding, philologically gifted thinker, who inspired people like Nicolai Hartmann, Ernst Cassirer, Werner Jaeger, Georg Misch, and many others. I would say that as I ventured those first hesitating steps on my own path in research, I was really taking the path of Julius Stenzel, who was greatly admired by Wilamowitz [Ulrich von Wilamowitz-Moellendorff] as well as Natorp. In later years, unfortunately, Julius and I never met again personally. We exchanged letters, and he very respectfully offered a critique of my first book [published 1931] in a German literary journal. I had already critiqued his work repeatedly, but among scholars this was not necessarily offensive. Why was this so among the German university younger generation of that time? Well, doubtless a feeling of deep disillusionment played a role, a disillusionment after the defeat which political Germany had to live through a transition to a parliamentary democracy. Democracy was an imported product for which there had really been no preparation. We can see this phenomenon again today when we approach what is going on in the Balkans. In any case, it was like this for us: we sought a new orientation, and this was to a certain extent the Greek polis. Werner Jaeger, in particular, the follower of Wilamowitz in Berlin, exercised a great school-forming influence, by foregrounding the evolution of the Greek city-state, of course in a pedagogically biased conceptuality, which I never found to be persuasively evident, especially when he discussed the Greek Paideia [education].[3] Helmut Kuhn, one of my friends who was about the same age as I was, published a really excellent critique of the first volume of Jaeger's *Paideia* at that time in the journal *Kant-Studien*.[4] Kuhn showed how paradoxical it is that someone undertaking such a great work would of all things start out with how the Sophists' concepts were developed. Another thing I had learned from Heidegger that became very helpful to me at that time was that in words there already reside indications that point to the meaning of a concept [*Begriffsanzeigen*]. So when one encounters *ousia*, the Greek word for being, in Aristotle and finds him saying that this word means, first of all, *real estate*, what is present, a capacity, the farm that the farmer has, then one begins to think more concretely. Thus I would say that, ultimately, thinking consists in realizing that the abstractions one performs can also be found in what is concretely real: concretizing is ultimately the soul of abstracting. I believe [Wolfgang] Schadewaldt confronted the essence of the matter when he later formulated it with persuasively naive enthusiasm: "We lack the *polis!*" In this he believed that he had found the most dreadful thing that could happen.

M O S T : Would you say, then, that the Greeks functioned in the twenties as a kind of critique of democracy, and thus they could be used in the quest for those socially binding values that were not adequately present in the form of parliamentary democracy?

G A D A M E R : I would rather say the real problem was that the political form was not filled with concretely real content, and for this reason one had first to persuade the intelligentsia, who had previously enjoyed a certain liberal freedom from politics, that we needed to find new solidarities within our society. So I would say it was not really a critique of democracy, as such, but more [the problem lay in] the knowledge that we could not yet do it.

M O S T : So, in the end, this is part of your thinking about our modernity.

G A D A M E R : Yes, indeed. In this sense it is something we keenly felt. But what was for me tremendously important, above all, was that through my philological teacher, Friedländer—but also strengthened through Stefan George and his circle—I found an artistic access to the writings of Plato. Through this, I very early became conscious of the limits of the concept-formation in our Western metaphysics. When I [later] decided to focus first of all on practical philosophy, it was above all because its impulses that had reached me from elsewhere, for example from the works of Dostoevsky or Kierkegaard, were also strongly present there.

M O S T : In your studies you started out with Plato, but you said you did not accomplish especially good results there. Then came Aristotle as a kind of making amends to Greek philosophy. Can one see in your work at that time and in the decades since then, a tension between what Plato has meant to you and what Aristotle has meant to you?

G A D A M E R : I certainly did not clearly recognize this at the time, because I was too strongly under the influence of Heidegger. And with all my admiration for that incomparably great thinker, I still have to say that while his getting back to a nonscholasticized Aristotle was a truly brilliant accomplishment, he was not equally successful in causing the completely different Platonic writings, drenched as they were with art, to *speak*. So at the start certainly I was a stronger follower of Aristotle than I later could be, or wanted to be in the long run. At that time I imagined to myself that Plato as yet saw things in a conceptually unsharp way, which Aristotle then transformed into the language of concepts. Fortunately, I later saw that Aristotle was not really so very different from Plato; his motives and impulses were not far from those found lodged in Platonic and Greek culture in general. Aristotle was not some Macedonian barbarian; rather, he belonged in the Platonic world.

M O S T : Precisely the claim and impact of Heidegger in the twenties and after shows that the concreteness achieved through the philological explication of words could be brought together with the abstractness of philosophical investigation in a very exciting (if also often quite problematic) way. Have you found in your own work that philosophical and philological investigation can be mutually enhancing?

G A D A M E R : Yes, I have felt this very strongly, above all in the inner attunement between the philological art of interpretation and the phenomenological clarity and intuitive vividness with which Heidegger, in spite of all his willfulness, raised philosophical language to an unbelievable level of suggestive power. Through this we were weaned from the innocence—or better, the anachronism—of the scholastic network of concepts. We now tried to approach things in their immediacy, and Aristotle, through gift and inclination, no less than Plato offered this to me. So suddenly the new task for me was to be able to think Aristotle *to-*

gether with Plato. And if one is trying to bring the matter to greater clarity, which one is continually impelled to do, then one will not be seeking some secret doctrine that is perhaps hidden somewhere, a teaching which can, when found, be deciphered by our colleagues in Tübingen; rather, one is persuaded that Plato himself knew what he was doing when, according to Aristotle, he introduced as his highest principle not the One only, but the One and an undetermined twoness, a twoness that requires ever new differentiations. And what he intended by this is certainly not a Neoplatonic transcendence. How one is supposed to understand the Good and the Beautiful as the One without the Many is certainly a mystery that one could never penetrate without Aristotle.

M O S T : So would you see it as characteristic of philosophical research that the better one understands the Greek philosophers historically, the better one can understand them philosophically?

G A D A M E R : I owe it to my good name as a hermeneut to say that of course it is only through concrete philological–historical knowledge and hermeneutical perspective that one also gains insights into the subject-matter. This means, for example, that one must consider what one is able to say in a writing for beginners, for instance in a *Protreptikos* [exhortation to study philosophy], and know how this differs from what one can and must write in dialogue form, and, further, what one is able to say only in living conversation. How could you possibly place these these on the same level with, say, two sentences from books by modern philosophers? Or how can one really hope to reconstruct the unity of what we call the "Aristotelian system"? All the ideas about system that have been applied to ancient times are absolutely anachronistic in relation to an age in which rhetoric and not literature played the leading role.

M O S T : With your reference to rhetoric and to the readership for which one writes, you have not only brought up an important hermeneutical category but also perhaps touched on a difference between Greek philosophers and modern philosophers. The Greek philosophers were certainly not university professors writing for other university professors. The Greek philosophers all wrote *Protreptikoi*, that is, writings of exhortation designed to attract people to philosophy. And each of them, at least up to the Epicureans, tried as philosophers, each in his own way, to intervene in the life of the state. Do you see a danger for philosophy today in the fact that it has become very professionalized and encapsulated, and relates only to itself?

GADAMER : Yes, this can be a real danger for several reasons. At the present moment, it looks as if we in Germany in the period since the Second World War and finally after a certain apprenticeship, understandably want to march forward to the drumbeat of the conquering nations; and you will find that those listening to that drumbeat interest themselves in analytic philosophy. Ironically, it is regarded as the latest thing precisely at a time when in the very countries where these were first developed, namely Great Britain and of course America, other new horizons are opening up. In this sense I would indeed say that today you find a very special kind of professionalism in German philosophy, and it is perhaps typical that Germany perennially arrives too late in this kind of competition among nations.

MOST : It is well known that there is not just *one* Greek philosophy but many different Greek philosophies, and one observes that various national lines in today's philosophy tend to feel that one part or another of Greek philosophy is particularly interesting and fruitful. For example, Hellenistic philosophy attracts the English and Americans who are above all interested in arguments, just as a short time ago a German philosophy oriented to wise sayings and deep things was drawn to the Presocratics. Where would you place your own philosophical work in this international panorama?

GADAMER : It is not so very easy to place myself within such a general framework at all. We philosophers are caught up in a constantly shifting exchange back and forth. If, as an old man now, I try to put forward just now how I view the latest developments (an old man who, so to say, views certain new currents with uneasiness, and who perhaps may say something unusual), I do note a certain tendency held in common between analytic philosophy and my own efforts, namely in philosophizing we both seek to link up with originary experiences. Of course, I believe these originary experiences are given not just in "ordinary language" but still more in the high forms of poetic language and in the literary tradition. So I can't imagine my own philosophizing not standing in a very intimate relationship to poetic texts in my mother tongue, and also to

French and English lyric poetry. And self-evidently also not without a close relationship to Greek poetry and philosophy.

M O S T : Your most important hermeneutical concepts are many times developed in close interaction with Aristotle. I mention only the concept of *phronesis* in this connection. At the same time, you have always been drawn to Plato. Is this because of the artistic side of Plato? Is it that in Plato art—the muses, the aesthetic—has a far more immediate presence than it does in Aristotle?

G A D A M E R : Yes—at least if you say that when one trains one's artistic powers, you also include in this that one makes gains in thinking, too. So I would say, yes, the concept of *phronesis*, that of practical rationality in Aristotle, has in fact attained a certain presence in my writings, but in accordance with the subject-matter I have repeatedly found impulses in this direction also in Plato. My work on the *Philebus* and the *Statesman* was not irrelevant in this regard; on the contrary, these writings served as very decisive preparations. As far as I can tell, Aristotle himself had the same thing in mind when he used the term *phronesis* not just in cases where one can simply measure things, and not only in the way Max Planck calls a fact "something you can measure," but rather in the sense that there is a "measure" that the things themselves possess.

M O S T : Perhaps the central point in the history of Greek philosophy is for you the transition from Plato to Aristotle. Yet you are also well acquainted with the Presocratics and with late Greek philosophy as well. I know that very recently you have occupied yourself with Plotinus. So I would ask: What has Greek philosophy other than Plato and Aristotle taught you above all?

G A D A M E R : Well, I am not being especially original when I say that Plato and Aristotle have taught me to understand the Presocratics. For what we call the Presocratics derives from what Plato and Aristotle knew about them. What the Presocratics themselves perhaps were, and out of what oriental, Egyptian, or Babylonian cultural heritages they ultimately blazed the path for the West to mathematics, logic, and science —all are things we learn to see in the Presocratics if we grasp that we have Plato and Aristotle to thank for the fact that we know anything about these at all.

M O S T : And Hellenistic philosophy—Epicurus, the Stoics, Neo-platonism—do you find these useful for your philosophy?

G A D A M E R : I must admit that late Hellenistic philosophy had a much stronger meaning for me in relation to my study of the New Testament. Still, I did devote a whole semester [the winter semester of 1930–31] to a course on Epictetus. Why? Because it struck me that Protestant theology, with which I maintained a very close relationship, lived in a much stronger but not fully understood dependence on the late Stoics that I did not fully understand. Also, I had a hunch that Stoic philosophy might be the secret popular philosophy of the natural scientific culture of our world.

M O S T : Then you see no inconsistency or contradiction between Greek philosophy and modern natural science?

G A D A M E R : Philosophy can never be in contradiction with science so long as philosophy remains science [*Wissenschaft*]. But a philosophy that only wants to be theory of science, obviously mistakes what it is, and a man of science who wants to "remain true to the earth" is really a Stoic without knowing it. So I think we can only really see a contradiction when we don't want to consider the matter carefully. For the most part, what hides behind the presumed contradictions is something that ultimately reconfirms the unity of reason [*Vernunft*]. Discovering contradictions is a good weapon for a lazy reason. I don't have a very high opinion of the denials of the unity of reason that have become stylish in this age of narrowed rational perspectives. I believe that people who are convinced that everything is embroiled in contradictions do not see far enough beyond their own contradictions.

M O S T : The Greeks never doubted the unity of reason. There are philosophers today, however, who see what is "modern" precisely in being doubtful about the unity of reason.

G A D A M E R : This is what in fact amazes me in the Nietzsche revival, both in France and in the rest of the world. With the rich cultural heritage that we have, it [the Nietzsche revival] still creates all these tensions today that people believe we have not resolved.

M O S T : Some of the most important German physicists of the twentieth century have gone back again and again to Greek philosophy. One begins to ask oneself to what degree the formation of their theories in physics has been influenced by their familiarity with Greek philosophy. What contribution do you think Greek philosophy has made to modern physics?

G A D A M E R : This is in fact a highly interesting phenomenon, which is connected, of course, with the unknown quotients [*Unbekanntheitsquotienten*], and they in turn are linked with the word "Pythagorean." If only we knew all this, then most probably a more precise answer could be given. But there is no doubt that modern science is inconceivable without the miracle of numbers, without "undetermined twoness" [referred to above]. Thus there also can be no doubt that our whole image of the world, and also the turn to mathematics [in modernity], rests on the Greek view of a numerically harmonious world. In spite of the turn of modern science to the instrumental employment of mathematics, research today still remains oriented to the Greek visions of a simplicity, unity, and beauty of the world, a world ordered and regulated in itself. Essentially, I grew up with physicists, and I still recall exactly that when I began my own studies such a total antithesis existed [between philosophy and science] that my father always said I would never be able to enter into a rational conversation with natural scientists at all.

M O S T : For you, then, the Greeks seem to form a vanishing point at which the unity of natural science, ethics, and aesthetics, as objects of reason, could be rescued. But in today's culture the subdivided realms of knowledge fall apart, and at the same time the Greeks are increasingly disappearing as a basis for our culture. Do you see other possible resources than the Greeks that would be able to preserve the rational unity of these and other realms?

G A D A M E R : In spite of all this, it is also the case today that the modern world is gradually coming together into a functional unity through science and technology, although this is taking place against the backdrop of highly different cultural centers and forms. We still do not really know anything about what our civilization with its skyscrapers and powerful machines means for human beings living in other parts of the world. Who knows, perhaps we will come to see that the relaxed conversation of a Chinese wise person with his disciples also has something to contribute, something that is quite different from the logic and desire for proof we first learned from the Greeks and which we have developed into an instrument to dominate the world and thereby perhaps have also disfigured [*denaturiert*] it.

M O S T : Our conversation has gotten closer and closer to the topic of art. Do you, along with Hölderlin, think that art could be the realm capable of guaranteeing the unity of all our endeavors?

G A D A M E R : I would agree at least in the sense that the philosophical formulations and conceptual means with which we think, clearly must always stand the test of art. Schelling once said that art is the *organon* [tool, instrument] of philosophy. By this he was saying that the *organon* of philosophy was not logic. In the West, philosophy is a distinguishing mark of our Greek heritage and it has been continually operative as a great tradition in its ultimate ramifications right up to the present day. Philosophy has been pursued in almost all cultural worlds, but we should still not delude ourselves that *philosophy*—and with it science and logic—alone really governs our orientation to the world and the formation of our souls. Rather, from earliest times religious messages have done this, and these find expression above all in the answers that the arts have put forward again and again to the ultimate questions of human existence. For example, in the nineteenth century, after the great tradition of metaphysics came to an end, the novel emerged as the new genre of world literature and became to a large extent the unifying bond for us. Today we read the books of García Márquez, we read Chinese and Japanese novels, and these suddenly have a new saying-power, a power in the period since the nineteenth century to break down our Eurocentrism, if you will; and this begins to expand and to bring about greater breadth for us in other dimensions. These are an important testimony to the fact that we need not view ourselves as merely puzzling exceptions. Reciprocally, within less than a hundred years, the east Asiatic high cultures have become admirers of German classical music. That must surely mean something. Indeed, it suggests that perhaps there is more unity today than disunity.

M O S T : From a philosophical standpoint, this also offers a justification of art. In the past few years American philosophers have begun to rediscover that art, especially literature, can have philosophical interest in terms of the ethical problems that arise in its presentation and performance. So perhaps Hegel's verdict, that art has finally achieved its highest form and thus is a thing of the past, must itself be superseded [*aufge-hoben*].

G A D A M E R : This verdict of Hegel has for the most part been a bit misused. What Hegel really meant was that while the Greek gods were present to the Greeks in visible forms, in the Christian tradition this is no longer the case. Also not in Judaism. Ultimately our culture starts out with a prohibition of images. But as the different requirements for life on this planet come together, I believe that unifying experiences will slowly increase and we will reach something like solidarities. Indeed, it is simply a bad joke today to make ecology a problem purely in relation to the national economy. And the same is true with many other things. Ulti-mately, peace and security cannot be achieved through the abolition of weapons by any individual country. To do this would probably only lead to war.

M O S T : It is just as much a bad joke to speak of a purely "German" philosophy or a purely "Italian" philosophy. Philosophy in the coming decades can contribute to causing the internationalization of world cul-ture to go on before our eyes as sympathetically as possible. What role in this do you see for Greek philosophy in particular?

G A D A M E R : Probably it will play a very significant role, because I know of no substitute for the immediate conceptual power of Greek as a spoken language. All modern languages of international exchange [*Ver-kehrsprachen*, linguae Francae] are becoming bland; their unique edges are being sanded down. The countries that have not yet been forced into this sanding down have had no means of communication with the outside world—for example, the black Congolese had to learn another language. These are highly intelligent people who in accordance with their tradi-tion, so to speak, seek the possibility of grasping the world in words, pic-tures, and concepts. I believe we in the West should go back once again to see the fateful way in which from a great beginning we find ourselves now driven to a point that is dangerously one-sided. And Western phi-losophy has played its part in this, also. I am no prophet, but I would think that by means of language and its possibility of creating solidarity in our mobile world, we will again and again discover points of solidarity. And then we will no longer need an ethics commission.

M O S T : Does this mean that precisely because ancient Greek is a dead language, Greek philosophy remains young and fresh? Does this mean that only if we in the Western tradition go back to drink from those healthy wellsprings and think them through again, can we perhaps become less dangerous to the rest of the world?

GADAMER: Perhaps. But perhaps there are also things in the traditions of ancient India or ancient China that will rival our tradition, and discovering this will also be a good thing for the ancient Greek sources!

MOST: Yes, that would indeed be fortunate. I thank you, Professor Gadamer.

ON PHENOMENOLOGY

with Alfons Grieder

Translation by Alfons Grieder

G R I E D E R :[1] Let us first talk about your way into philosophy, and particularly into *phenomenology*. We do not have to adhere too rigorously in this case to the question and answer pattern, I think.

G A D A M E R : To begin with, let me tell you how I first heard of phenomenology. It was after the First World War, in Marburg.[2] There we had among us an art historian, Richard Hamann, who was very progressive and with whose encouragement we ran one of those debating societies which students—even older ones—tend to be fond of in times of social upheaval.[3] And each of us had his recipe for putting the world in order again: somebody was telling us about Max Weber, another about Stefan George, yet another about . . . I do not remember . . .

G R I E D E R : Marx, perhaps?

G A D A M E R : Yes, somebody may have mentioned Marx. After all, it was in 1919–20. But, then after much discussion, somebody said: "Only phenomenology can help us." I pricked up my ears. It was a certain Mr. Nöggerath who said this. He was of course known in Husserlian circles, as I heard later, and was one of those of whom one may say, with Goethe:

Und zuletzt, des Lichts begierig
Bist du, Schmetterling, verbrannt.[4]
[And in the end, eager for light,
You, butterfly, are burned up.]

He was one who was burnt up in the light of phenomenology, so to speak: nothing ever came of him. On this occasion, then, I heard the word "phenomenology" for the first time. Then I began to inquire a bit further. A student of Natorp's explained Husserl's *Ideas*[5] in a private colloquium for two or three people, including myself. These ideas became even more obscure with my private reading of Husserl. In 1922 I went to Freiburg, with with purpose in mind of inquiring further. I had completed my Ph.D. under Natorp,[6] too early of course; it was no good.

GRIEDER: You were only twenty-two!

GADAMER: Yes. After a war there is always a kind of shadow in which one can sometimes make an early career. In any case, such was the path which led me to phenomenology. Nicolai Hartmann was very keen on phenomenology, and so was Natorp, of course, who was in fact one of the precursors of the Husserlian idealistic turn. It was Natorp's concept of a general psychology which forced Husserl to relax the position he took in the *Logical Investigations* and to take account of what, in the meantime, has become known as *passive synthesis*, or, as Natorp expressed it in his more primitive terminology: the ideas themselves must be in motion. Already as a student I was thinking about this but without really coming to grips with it. Of course, Plato's *Sophist*, a dialogue with which I was already somewhat familiar, provided a clue. However, even before that I had been inspired by reading the manuscript of Heidegger's essay, "Anzeige der hermeneutischen Situation," which has just recently been published [1992] in the *Dilthey-Jahrbuch*.[7] The most important Heideggerian text to have appeared posthumously is this earliest work of his to which I have recently written an introduction.[8] Here we have a project showing the young Heidegger on his way to Aristotle and Plato. It is quite clear that Heidegger's whole life was the life of a God-seeker. He had been given a Catholic education, and he was of course a philosophically minded man, suffering painfully under the prevailing neo-Thomism, an incredible mixture of St. Thomas and Kant. He liberated himself through his reading of Kierkegaard and Dilthey, and with the help of Husserl himself. Through Husserl he acquired the appropriate technique (if one may call it that), the conscientiousness of phenomenological description.

G R I E D E R : What attracted you most, as a philosopher, in phenomenology?

G A D A M E R : The answer is simple. I went to Husserl's seminar, and when people spoke in a high-sounding manner he said: "Not always the big notes! Small change, gentlemen!" I am the son of a natural scientist; I too dislike empty talk.

G R I E D E R : In phenomenology you found a certain sort of scientific attitude, an emphasis on piecemeal work.

G A D A M E R : And concreteness! Still today people say of my work in philosophy that it makes things concrete.

G R I E D E R : Indeed. It is very accessible also for English readers, and in a sense in which Heidegger's writings are not and even Husserl's are sometimes not.

G A D A M E R : Here another factor comes into play. As a speaker Heidegger was quite understandable.

G R I E D E R : Yes, one is astonished when one reads his lectures, the discrepancy—

G A D A M E R : Of course, his lectures are quite different. They can be understood, and certainly understood better than his later writings. I had predicted that this would be the case with Heidegger as it was with Hegel, who surely did not become famous through his *Logic* but rather through his lectures.

G R I E D E R : I keep encouraging my students to consult Hegel's Berlin lectures, for this very reason. Admittedly, his rigorous logic is not always conspicuous in them, and Hegel often speaks more in allusions. And the same seems to apply to Heidegger—

G A D A M E R : Yes, basically the same, very similar. Well then, I was eager to get to know Heidegger, and he really took care of me, in Freiburg, where he was Husserl's assistant. He invited me to his home—as I briefly described in my autobiography.[9] And then he introduced me a little to his reading of Aristotle, which was in fact a phenomenological reading of Aristotle. Indeed, Heidegger's masterstroke was that he convinced Husserl that Aristotle was the first phenomenologist prior to Husserl.

GRIEDER: I sometimes feel that in those days you were perhaps more attracted by Heidegger the interpreter, the phenomenological interpreter, than by the central doctrines of Husserlian phenomenology.

GADAMER: You are perfectly right. Of course, as far as Husserl's philosophy was concerned, I was not quite up to it. I was twenty-three when I got to know Husserl himself. I attended his seminars. I was attracted. It was rather curious, and one episode I remember rather well: at the beginning of one of these seminars Husserl asked a question, and at first nobody answered. Finally I decided to reply to it. And Husserl takes my answer up, goes into it and talks for one and a half hours, without full stops or commas. Then the bell sounds. He stands up with Heidegger and his other assistants, and he turns to Heidegger with the words: "Today we really had an interesting discussion, for a change."

GRIEDER: Well, was he not a monological thinker?

GADAMER: Later Heidegger also became monological. The early Heidegger, however, was not like that at all, but rather as I tried my whole life to remain: ready to listen to the other, to respond to him or her.

GRIEDER: But did he respond discursively? I mean, was there debate, discussion for and against?

GADAMER: "Debate" would not be quite the right expression. Let me give you an example! We were all sitting together in Heidegger's Aristotle seminar, in Freiburg, the first course of his I attended. Somehow we began to talk about the practical sense, practical reason. Making my own contribution I said: "One must be able to *see*." My remark was immediately taken up by Heidegger: "Why does Dr. Gadamer say 'to see'? Please see *Nicomachean Ethics*, Book VI, ὄμμα τῆς ψυχῆ [the eye of the soul]!"[10] This is how he was in those days, he took up a student's points in a positive way.

Here's another wonderful story: Heidegger was in charge of the pro-seminar, which he had to conduct for Husserl. He had convinced "the old one" (as he used to say) that only the *Logical Investigations* should be dealt with there, and not the *Ideas*. Of the latter he did not want to hear at all. The Sixth Investigation was of course particularly dear to him. "*He* has the 'ideas'; *we* first have to come to terms with the *Logical Investiga*-

tions," Heidegger used to say,[11] thus evading the conflict, as he bypassed one conflict after another until he was faced with one he unfortunately failed to bypass.

He used to ask questions like, for instance, "Who saw for the first time what the concrete-individual really is?" Various answers were suggested, for example, that it was Leibniz. "He would have been glad to know this," Heidegger replied, "but it was in fact Husserl."

This is how it all started. But then—you are quite right—I became a classical philologist, because Heidegger's superiority was such that I had to say to myself: "Now you have to learn something which he doesn't know." And thus, under Friedländer's[12] guidance, I became a classical philologist and played an influential role in that field, as you may know. In fact, my essay on the *Protrepticus* turned the whole Jaegerian Aristotle conception upside down, did it not?[13]

G R I E D E R : And Jaeger was quite an authority in those days.

G A D A M E R : Very much so.

G R I E D E R : Now a question concerning Husserl: Am I right in thinking that already at that time in Freiburg you were anything but happy and at ease with the Husserlian transcendental turn?

G A D A M E R : Inwardly, I had already done away with it for quite some time. After all, I had been reading Dilthey. Already the old Natorp was getting close to what I was to elaborate later. Heidegger commented, "You never quite got rid of your teacher Natorp." I think this was on the occasion of my seventieth birthday. I recall that in a letter (not written to me) the old Natorp wrote: "Finally I have found the ground and basis."

G R I E D E R : What was this ground?

G A D A M E R : Language! Not only in England after 1936, after Hitler's violation of the Munich treaty, were philosophers disposed towards a linguistic turn, but also within the phenomenological movement itself.[14]

G R I E D E R : And connected with this is another similarity: the return to piecemeal work, to the "small change" referred to earlier. We also find it in Russell and Wittgenstein, as a return to detailed work of a logical or linguistic nature.

G A D A M E R : Of course. I keep saying it again and again. In some as yet unpublished writings I showed repeatedly what these inner connections between the two movements are. However, one has to know English very well in order to come to terms with analytic philosophy. My English is not quite good enough. One needs a feel for the nuances of the language. I am of the opinion, however, that close relations are possible here.[15] And I would say that we were more successful with our phenomenological method, with our endeavor to return to the intuitively given and to the concrete. Whether this was due to our imaginativeness or the lack of it I shall leave open. In my teaching too I proceed in that way—you witnessed it yourself—always giving concrete examples to make things comprehensible.

GRIEDER: And yet it has to be pointed out that both Husserl and Heidegger left the concrete and intuitively given behind, in a sense. Heidegger concerns himself with Being, and Husserl with the "acts" and structures of the "stream of consciousness." This seems to have frightened many analytic philosophers off, not just Ryle. Hence in Heidegger as well as in Husserl a nonintuitive element turns up. Husserl thought these structures of transcendental consciousness to be intuitively given; but many maintain that they are not.

GADAMER: To some extent he was right. Husserl's analyses of inner time-consciousness are intuitive-concrete.[16]

GRIEDER: No doubt, in some respect they are. However, one may argue that Husserl in fact brings in some hypotheses, for example about continuity and retention, which go beyond the intuitively given. There is a certain tension between Husserl's professed phenomenological-intuitive approach and his claims about inner time-consciousness.

GADAMER: Sometimes he could be very concrete-intuitive; for example, when he described an experience as follows: "One day in Berlin I went to the Panopticum. As I came up the stairs behind the Friedrichstrasse a lady smiled at me in such a friendly manner, and I stepped forward towards her: it was a puppet." This experience he presented as an example of the crossing out of a protention. He was able to present such a story almost like an actor. Heidegger did not have this ability to the same degree, but artistically he was more gifted. Heidegger's language and style had a certain plastic power—boorish, barbarian, admittedly—like an elephant going through the primeval forest. My style is unfortunately not as powerful as Heidegger's, but it is smoother. He spoke South

German dialect, whereas I came from Silesia, where not one word of dialect was allowed. In Husserl, who spoke an Austrian dialect, one notices the style of the Habsburg bureaucracy.

Regarding Heidegger, I may add that in the early years of the Third Reich, I avoided him. His political engagement was too embarrassing to me. Not that I blamed him; every human being may err. But I did not want to be recommended by him.

G R I E D E R : Ah! You did not obtain the chair in Leipzig through Heidegger's recommendation?[17]

G A D A M E R : Not at all! I was never a member of the Party and was not politically active. At Leipzig I had the special fortune that Heisenberg was interested in my publications on ancient atomic theory.[18] He was a man with sufficient authority—against the Party. This is how I got the call to Leipzig: the members of staff in philosophy there, some of them pupils of Heidegger, wanted me, and Heisenberg gave his approval. I was told that when the discussion turned to me somebody remarked: "Gadamer is a very sportive man." However, another person present objected, pointing out that this could not be right, as Gadamer had had poliomyelitis. Then Heisenberg intervened and said that contrary to a widespread prejudice one did not play tennis with one's feet, but with one's head.

II

G R I E D E R : *Truth and Method* contains a chapter entitled "Overcoming the Epistemological Problem through Phenomenological Research" (*GW* 1: 192–213, Part II). The title refers to Dilthey's epistemological way of posing the hermeneutic problem. It is this epistemological approach which, in your view, should be overcome. Dilthey's problem concerns the possibility of historical experience and historical knowledge. Now students, confronted with your criticism as set forth in that chapter, are sometimes puzzled and ask: "What's wrong with Dilthey's [work with the] epistemological problem? Is it not a perfectly legitimate problem? Gadamer may have chosen another line of research, and perhaps a very fruitful one; but from this it does not follow that the problem Dilthey posed was an illegitimate one."

G A D A M E R : To this I would answer most decidedly as follows. So long as we are concerned with the natural sciences, one can have a theory of knowledge or a theory of science. But when we are dealing with the "life-world," as Husserl calls it, and with the *Geisteswissenschaften*, then the scientific concept of knowledge only allows us to know the boring.

G R I E D E R : Still, we get to know *something*.

G A D A M E R : This I do not deny at all. I am not at all against method. I merely maintain that it is not the only route of access to knowledge. How could I be opposed to method? I am a classical philologist, who knows quite well what methods are, and thus what a theory of knowledge is. But Dilthey was searching for something else.

G R I E D E R : The *Sinnzusammenhang* [context of meaning], for instance.

G A D A M E R : The possibility of grasping this kind of context could not be made intelligible by means of an epistemology [theory of knowledge] that was modelled on the natural sciences.

G R I E D E R : In *Truth and Method* you point out that there was a certain tension in Dilthey, an inconsistency almost, between a philosophy of life and the scientific means he employs—

G A D A M E R : —his methodological concern, due to John Stuart Mill and the British Empiricists, and then the excessive NeoKantian freight.

G R I E D E R : So, to get further there had first to be a break, an *ontological* rupture as you describe it in your book.

G A D A M E R : Precisely.

G R I E D E R : This rupture occurred through Heidegger, I assume.

G A D A M E R : Essentially it was due to Heidegger. It then manifested itself in Georg Misch, Dilthey's son-in-law.

G R I E D E R : In his book *Lebensphilosophie und Phänomenologie*, for instance?[19]

G A D A M E R : Indeed, there the Heideggerian influence already asserted itself. And so I would reply to people such as the students you just mentioned: Why do the historical sciences interest us? Surely not because they are sciences, but because they tell us something that is philosophically relevant, that is, regarding questions that do not concern controlling some field of objects.

I therefore maintain that we have to concern ourselves, as philoso-

phers, with the voice of poetry, and to be near poetry and the arts generally, as was already emphasized by Schelling in German Idealism. This I
have done throughout my life. The volume of my collected works which
is at the printers right now [*GW* 9 (1993)] contains nothing but interpretations of poetry.

G R I E D E R : These involve cultural relationships quite different
from the ones prevailing in analytic philosophy.

G A D A M E R : [This represents] a totally different relationship to
language.

G R I E D E R : May we go back to the ontological rupture, the rediscovery of being, of Dasein, of the being of humans and the being of history?

G A D A M E R : The point is of course that "being" is a verb, an insight Heidegger had arrived at only very slowly; but in *Being and Time* the
insight is there.

G R I E D E R : The meaning of being—to be determined through the
time-horizon, the ecstases. As I see it, the fulcrum of *Truth and Method*
was another one: the notion of understanding [*Verstehen*]. Indeed one
may be surprised how little use you made of certain key terms of *Being
and Time* like *Befindlichkeit* [how one finds oneself, attunement], which
was still important to Heidegger during the 1930s, in the Hölderlin lectures, for example.[20]

G A D A M E R : I always tried to avoid the Heideggerian terminology. This is what Heidegger himself basically wanted: that each student
should find his or her own words. I of course count myself among Heidegger's students. But I say this: Do not imitate Heidegger; let yourself
be inspired by him!

G R I E D E R : Let us take the Heideggerian notion of understanding
as "thrown projection" [*geworfener Entwurf*], to which you also refer.

G A D A M E R : "Thrownness" [*Geworfenheit*] is, I think, a peripheral
concept, meant to underline the facticity of *Dasein*. In *Truth and Method* I
do not talk about "*Geworfenheit*" but about tradition.

G R I E D E R : And also custom, which has much to do with the Heideggerian drawing from the possibilities *Dasein*, the being that has been
[*gewesenes Dasein*].

G A D A M E R : Of course, of course!

GRIEDER: This is an important point of contact, perhaps easily overlooked by those who know little of *Being and Time*.

GADAMER: Oh yes, this is my Heideggerian basis. I should point out, however, that I did not attempt what the later Heidegger was after: to forcibly recast language, so to speak. This is not language any more, I said to myself. True, one always searches in language for the right word. Yet it is not the word which is decisive, but the whole process of communication. I am not at all obliged to say things once and for all in a single word. It is sufficient that the other person has understood. This was *my* way—I told Heidegger that language is not the powerful word; rather, language is reply.

GRIEDER: Let us for a moment return to understanding and the famous hermeneutic circle, a theme you took up in *Truth and Method*.[21] The circular structure involves two heterogeneous elements, it seems to me. One of these one finds in all scientific research, also in the natural sciences: one projects some hypothesis, which one then tries to confirm or refute. In the case of refutation one has to modify one's hypothesis. Thus, you speak of a whole of meaning [*Sinnganzen*] which is projected. Once it is projected, one may try to confirm it, for example, by interpreting a text.

GADAMER: Now when one is doing mathematical physics it is different: one does provide proofs.

GRIEDER: "Proofs" that rest on certain presuppositions. Already in the 1930s Gaston Bachelard and Ferdinand Gonsoeth worked with the idea that theories in the so-called exact sciences are tentatively projected and that there is discontinuous development in the sciences through a series of radical theoretical reorganizations. It seems Thomas S. Kuhn did not know about the work Bachelard and Gonsoeth had already done. But back to the circular structure, its two elements—[22]

GADAMER: Evidently, there is this first element.

GRIEDER: Then there is a second one. You pointed out in *Truth and Method* that all understanding contains an irreducible temporal, historical condition: facticity, the situation. It prescribes certain limits, and ultimately one moves in a circle determined by the historical horizon.

GADAMER: Heidegger took up the issue of the hermeneutic circle which was already addressed in Plato's *Phaedrus*. If I want to understand, then I must project something, and one must return to the project again and again. This is the first element, which you described. But now to the second element: this is the one I emphasized. Hence my notion of play. One *participates* in play as a partner. Some people speak of it as "the hermeneutic method," but a method is precisely what it is *not*.

G R I E D E R : According to your view, it is rather the being of history one is dealing with. In the end it comes down to the fusion of horizons.

G A D A M E R : Which *happens* to us, of course, and is not at all of our own making.

G R I E D E R : You sometimes say that to understand one has to project an historical horizon. In projecting something one is already in a finite historical situation, and the historical conditioning is already in play. Thus, even the first projection seems mediated.

G A D A M E R : The fusion is primary, of course.

G R I E D E R : And then it goes from mediation to mediation.

G A D A M E R : This is precisely how I presented it.

G R I E D E R : The series of mediations is analogous to the movement in Hegel's *Phenomenology of Mind*. Except that in Hegel one moves in the direction of absolute knowledge. Now I would like to raise another issue, if we still have a little time for it.

G A D A M E R : Please.

G R I E D E R : You were born in 1900, the year when the phenomenological movement began, in a sense.

G A D A M E R : When it was initiated. It was a bit later, of course, that one began to speak of "phenomenology."

G R I E D E R : When you now look back over this period of time and this development, which has been contemporaneous with your own life, are you satisfied with it? Has phenomenology in your opinion achieved what you expected of it? Has its potential been realized?

G A D A M E R : I would say that there has been too much talk *about* phenomenology, and not enough phenomenological work. One does not always have to insist that what one is doing is phenomenology, but one ought to work phenomenologically, that is, descriptively, creatively–intuitively, and in a concretizing manner. Instead of simply applying concepts to all sorts of things, concepts ought to come forward in movements of thought springing from the spirit of language and the power of intuition. Such is my criticism of phenomenology. The founding fathers after Husserl—Max Scheler, Heidegger, perhaps also Adolf Reinach (this is difficult to judge as he was killed so young in the war), even Hans Lipps—were people who *practiced* phenomenology, who by virtue of phenomenology brought us all this new knowledge.[23] Yet they did not just talk about phenomenology and what it is.

GRIEDER: I'm sorry, but the way you are characterizing phenomenology strikes me as rather formal: return to the intuitive, bring out the intuitive contents in language. You are not characterizing it in terms of the more specific features of the Husserlian or Heideggerian approaches, that is, with reference to their basic concerns, such as the Husserlian description of the structure of transcendental consciousness or the Heideggerian hermeneutics of *Dasein* and its ecstases. You may of course insist that if one analyzes what this means, exhausting the intuitive content of language, then one comes back to something like Heideggerian temporality.

GADAMER: You asked whether I am satisfied with the phenomenological movement. My reply is this: Precisely not where it presents itself as some technical conceptual system and thus turns into scholasticism. Yet this is what happened to phenomenology, to some extent. The really productive people, such as Scheler, Heidegger, or Lipps, mobilized it again. And I too have attempted to do this in my own field and on the basis of my own inspirations. By studying poetry, the visual arts, architecture, and music I come to understand what Heidegger means by "nearness to being."

GRIEDER: So you see no contradiction between your work in phenomenology and Heidegger's?

GADAMER: No. When Heidegger expounds temporality and being as time, I am really with him. I can show this quite well in the case of the work of art: the work of art is speaking because we are listening. And what do I do as a listener? I am involved in a circular movement such as you described earlier. Yes, in a sense I do mean temporalization as Heidegger expounded it—with a certain conceptual boldness of his own.

GRIEDER: Nobody alive could have illuminated the phenomenological movement so much from the inside, and from such a rich personal experience as you did this afternoon. Thank you, Professor Gadamer, for this interview.

6

"THE REAL NAZIS HAD NO INTEREST AT ALL IN US..."

with Dörte von Westernhagen

(Prefatory note: During the period of German fascism what were the philosophers doing? For a long time, this question was applied only to notorious Nazis like Ernst Krieck, Alfred Baeumler, or Hans Heyse, and in this way it was excommunicated from the history of philosophy, except for the garden of errors in debates about Heidegger. Philosophical relationships in National Socialism, so far as the everyday business of academic research and teaching were concerned, have remained obscure. A short time ago, however, the situation began to change. Research projects on this topic have been undertaken and the first results have appeared in print. In her feature series of radio broadcasts at the end of 1989 under the title "Between Science and Worldview—Philosophy in the Third Reich" (Radio Bremen/Südwestfunk), Dörte von Westernhagen interviewed some still living witnesses from that period and through these interviews made information on this topic accessible to the wider public. Among these was her conversation with Hans-Georg Gadamer, which took place on July 4, 1989.)[1]

WESTERNHAGEN: In 1933 what professors of philosophy had to go?

GADAMER: One commonly pictures this process as something that took place all at once, but it was not not like this. For instance, a large number of my Jewish friends, almost all of whom fought in the First World War, were not suspended from their teaching duties in 1933. This came only some two or three years later.

WESTERNHAGEN: Someone who has researched this matter told me that half of all of those who in the course of these years had to go had already been sacked in 1933.

GADAMER: That is surely wrong. It may be the case in the government but not in the university. As is well known, Jewish colleagues who were suspended from their teaching continued to receive their full pay. And it was only little by little that they were suspended from teaching; only in 1936 were the Jewish participants in the First World War also suspended from teaching. I still remember very clearly that those who were full professors could stay on to pursue research. Those individuals all continued on until 1938.

WESTERNHAGEN: You took a temporary teaching position in Kiel in 1933–1934.[2] At this time Julius Stenzel and Richard Kroner had to go. Stenzel was compelled to move to a position at Halle University. What was the background for this? Was he politically unpopular?

GADAMER: There was a special situation behind this in Kiel. The Nazis intended to make Kiel a model nordic-racist university. But the whole Kiel school of jurisprudence was located there, followers of Carl Schmitt. The other instance was Richard Kroner. You are quite correct; he was Jewish.[3] By chance, I had been a very close friend of his, so it was a very emotional moment when we saw each other again because I was the Aryan who was suddenly chosen to occupy his place. My happiness there in Kiel was short-lived.

WESTERNHAGEN: We understand today that there were already a lot of chairs open there—

GADAMER: Yes, a whole series of chairs were vacant, but certain of these were on account of compelled displacements that took place in order to make way for major topics of their worldview, or what they may have thought they wanted there. This applied to the two chairs that were vacant [in the philosophy department] when I came to Kiel. One of them was filled by a Party sympathizer, Kurt Hildebrandt, a follower of [the poet Stefan] George,[4] and I received the other.

WESTERNHAGEN: In your autobiography [*Philosophische Lehrjahre* (*Philosophical Apprenticeships*)][5] you write that Hildebrandt was one of those "fine, innocent, and naive persons who was led astray by the political situation and his own ambition" [*PL* 53/*PA* 79]. Was he one of those young people who was given a professorship because he conformed to the party line and the NSDAP [*Nationalsozialistische Deutsche Arbeiterpartei*, or Nazi Party] expected that he would formulate a National-Socialist philosophy?

GADAMER: The followers of Stefan George were a special case. The George circle was a group with a conservative and nationalistic bias, half of whom were Jewish! So in 1933 the great rift came. Hildebrandt was a *Privatdozent* [an unsalaried university instructor], a psychiatrist—a highly educated man. In the 1920s he had written a very interesting book, *Norm and Degeneracy* [*Norm und Entartung*],[6] which one could profitably read today. It is a bit, well, George-istic. Is that a concept for you?—Solemn, a bit solemn and ceremonious.

WESTERNHAGEN: I can't get anything at all out of that high and hollow pathos.

GADAMER: That's too bad; a great loss for you.

WESTERNHAGEN: That may be.

GADAMER: There are wonderful poems of absolutely infinite value. "Harken to what the damp earth is saying/you, free as a bird or a fish/you don't know what it is you are suspended in/perhaps a later mouth will discover/you sat among us at our table/you ate from our store/indeed time grew old, today no man loves/you don't know whether he will ever come/he who can still see this face . . . " In those days, the reforms at Kiel were led by a rector who was a follower of Stefan George. This was typical of the conservative revolution in Kiel; they were not really Nazis. They all joined the Party or were already in it. This holds for Hildebrandt, who also came to Kiel in connection with this project. That I was called there surely also had to do with my connections with the George circle, which I was not a member of, but in which I had many friends. Max Kommerell was one of these friends. So this was a very idealistic conservative group.

WESTERNHAGEN: I would like to ask about the new arrivals there. Noack in Hamburg practically stepped into the shoes of Cassirer.[7]

GADAMER: He had slowly become eligible for it after many years.

WESTERNHAGEN: Or Heyse in Göttingen.

GADAMER: But these were late cases. Heyse was already a professor in Breslau and then came to Königsberg and only thereafter to Göttingen.[8]

WESTERNHAGEN: But this also happened in the mid-thirties.

GADAMER: No. Königsberg of course immediately became one of the targets of Nazi reconstruction; I would refer you to Walter F. Otto, for instance.[9] Königsberg was a dream of the East [reconstructing presumably the eastern part of Germany].

WESTERNHAGEN: Gehlen went there, also.[10]

GADAMER: Exactly. A people without enough space.

WESTERNHAGEN: Gehlen was also one of these new people who were brown [Nazi-friendly] enough and conservative enough. We do not really need to mention the decidedly Nazi philosophers like Krieck, Baeumler, and Grunsky, but rather the right-wing conservatives who took advantage of the moment in 1933.

GADAMER: You express it in a perhaps too unfriendly way; I would say: ones who actually allowed themselves be inspired by this constellation.

WESTERNHAGEN: You are right. I don't want to say that it was purely careerism, but rather—

GADAMER: I really don't think one ought to malign these people. Schelsky also belongs in this group of right-wing conservatives. Freyer was their main intellectual leader.

WESTERNHAGEN: And Rothacker?

GADAMER: I don't like to have to talk about his case. Quite frankly, I found him truly outrageous. He went into the propaganda ministry. I once heard a lecture he gave in Marburg. He said: "I would suggest that you introduce a *German* semester." All the different disciplines should make what was German the object of their studies for the whole semester. In addition, he noted, the German semester would give him a fine opportunity to observe the levels of enthusiasm of the professors as they carried it out. I found that really offensive.[11]

118

W E S T E R N H A G E N : And did he really discipline the people who were not zealous enough?

G A D A M E R : Oh yes, he denounced them! After that, I did not want to have anything to do with Rothacker. It is one thing to be an enthusiast, but that was real cynicism. Later, he was always very disappointed that I never responded to invitations from him when I was myself a professor, both before and after 1945.

W E S T E R N H A G E N : Now once again about the role of Freyer.

G A D A M E R : Freyer was not a member of the Party. He belonged to those right-wing conservatives who viewed with horror its path into barbarism, but cooperated because of the cultural–political program. Freyer was, so to speak, the noblest type of right-wing conservative revolutionary. Why he went to that cultural institute in Budapest, I do not know. But it is of course a fabrication to believe he went because he was afraid he could no longer remain in Leipzig. This is maintained by some of his disciples today. It is absurd.[12]

W E S T E R N H A G E N : Are the stories about Rothacker known among our contemporaries?

G A D A M E R : No, for that one had to have been there.

W E S T E R N H A G E N : The cultural-political proposals he made were shocking. He wanted to set up a Führer's university.

G A D A M E R : Exactly. Indeed, he strongly emphasized this. And a German semester! Really, it makes one's hair stand on end.

W E S T E R N H A G E N : What is so hard for people born after 1945 to understand is that he later became a teacher of Habermas and many other major philosophers, and they have always very much spared him from blame.

G A D A M E R : Yes, this also, of course. Rothacker was no dumbbell. And he did make a contribution. His book, *Introduction to the Geisteswissenschaften*, was a real accomplishment. He was a tremendously wide reader and an excellent moderator. That was his function in Bonn. Habermas, Apel, Ilting, Pöggeler, all these people were with Rothacker; but they learned from Oskar Becker.

W E S T E R N H A G E N : With Oskar Becker you are once again speaking of a completely doubtful case.

G A D A M E R : Exactly. He was a great scholar.

WESTERNHAGEN: And in 1933, if one follows Löwith's presentation of it, he was also one of those who fell [for Hitler] in March.[13]

GADAMER: He was never a member of the Party.

WESTERNHAGEN: And yet what about his ideas on the authoritarian Führer-state, or about the Jews being a misfortune for German culture?

GADAMER: Of course I could not agree with Becker at the time about that.

WESTERNHAGEN: Where did you at that time belong politically?

GADAMER: I would see myself not as a right-wing conservative but rather as a liberal. As were all my Jewish friends in Marburg. They were more or less nationalists, but of course they were liberals.

WESTERNHAGEN: In your autobiography you write that Becker was not an anti-Semite and he was unjustly cast out.

GADAMER: Of course Becker was a theorist about race, but a very good one, like his friend Ferdinand Clauss, also. The book by Clauss, *Seele und Rasse* [*Soul and Race*] was published in 1923, and there were no Nazis then.[14]

WESTERNHAGEN: This may lead us to place everything much earlier.

GADAMER: Excuse me, but races have existed since the creation of the world.

WESTERNHAGEN: Yes, but my question is how far had this already entered into the tradition of philosophy prior to 1933?

GADAMER: Really not at all. Clauss and Becker were outsiders, very free thinkers. This was the *Volkerpsychologie* [psychology of peoples] in the style of Wundt. There of course you do find the race problem. But you cannot make Becker into a Nazi because of his theory of race.

WESTERNHAGEN: For me it is hard to keep the two apart. Someone has race-theoretical ideas and allows them to enter into his philosophy, and yet you say he is no anti-Semite. When one reads what Löwith writes about his exchange of letters with Becker, one develops an abhorrence of the attitude of Becker.

GADAMER: I too felt that way when I read it. He also published something in the 1940s that I found very regrettable, because it seemed to have a brown coloration. At the same time, one must grant that his race-theoretical interests were completely legitimate. As thinking persons, why should we not try to understand what we have in the meantime begun to grasp: what Arabs are, what persons from India, Islam, China, and Tibet are? Really, all this is beyond the grasp of our European concepts. Isn't that a philosophical problem?

W E S T E R N H A G E N : I would agree that various cultural spheres may be regarded from religious/sociological and cultural/anthropological and other standpoints.

G A D A M E R : And these cultures have racial foundations.

W E S T E R N H A G E N : What?

G A D A M E R : The people of India are not Japanese.

W E S T E R N H A G E N : But when this is translated into political actions, such that the Germans took completely assimilated Western intellectuals who were no longer even regarded as Jewish and deported them on the basis of racial standpoints—

G A D A M E R : But nobody based it on that, not even Becker. Even my Jewish friends have said, "This will certainly have a bad end, this flood of people from the East, highly skilled businessmen." And Becker did not have the real scholars in mind, the Jews in the universities.

W E S T E R N H A G E N : For me it is a matter of needing to see that in the twenties there were certain patterns and currents of thought that were combinable with the Nazis' militant racial hatred.

G A D A M E R : Certainly not originally. We intellectuals regarded anti-Semites like Werner Butzbach as crazy. For you to act as if the philosophers would have played some kind of role in this anti-Semitism —you just can't do that. Rather, that was Hitler in Vienna.

W E S T E R N H A G E N : I do think that within the humanities and social sciences philosophers were a thread in the whole.

G A D A M E R : Writers and poets were much, much more important, of course, because they reached more people.

W E S T E R N H A G E N : Yes. But my point is that with regard to the topic of "Philosophy in the Third Reich" there are few publications that show us individual lines of development.

G A D A M E R : Any information I have I will be glad to share with you. I have already spoken about Rothacker, and at the same time also not been silent about his contributions. Even before '45 it was self-evident one could speak frankly with him. It was completely clear to me that he was rather cynical in his cooperation with the Nazis back in 1933–34. I do not at all doubt that he later regarded it as a mistake. There was no need for me to talk seriously with him about it.

WESTERNHAGEN: What do you mean by "later"?

GADAMER: When the war began [in 1938], at the latest. Up to the year 1938, knowing little about all these dreadful things he had done, one could as a German say: "Hitler achieved a brilliant politics of [international] blackmail: it was indeed masterful how he reconstructed the balance of power in Europe." But that it would lead to a war we asses did not see. I am describing this now in the very words that Erich Frank, a friend of Karl Jaspers, the possessor of the sofa on which you are sitting, used in talking to me.[15] But none of us gave lectures from the podium about a National-Socialistic worldview. None of us talked from the lectern about race. I would not even assume this about Becker.

WESTERNHAGEN: Didn't Hildebrandt write a book, *Plato: The Struggle of the Spirit for Power*?

GADAMER: He wrote this back in 1930. Books took three years to appear in print.

WESTERNHAGEN: OK. But this is an example of the fact that presumably many other philosophers also suddenly interpreted Plato in such a way that the state Plato imagined became a model for the National-Socialist state.

GADAMER: Here you are really underestimating the intelligence of us professors of philosophy! When this proposal appeared in Feder's[16] effort to establish the party line, we philosophers read about this with scornful laughter. What are you thinking of us?

WESTERNHAGEN: Let's drop the subject.

GADAMER: Yes, but I still must ask you quite plainly what you think of us? Do you really think we philosophers took seriously all this nonsense in relation to Plato?

WESTERNHAGEN: Weren't there several who took it in this way?

GADAMER: No. Even Baeumler, with his book about the Overman, would have been too smart to do that! No, this he would not have done.

WESTERNHAGEN: I must pester you once again about your own personal involvement: Somewhere I read that in November 1933 you signed that unspeakably awful "Appeal of the Saxon Nazi Teachers Union for the Reichstag Election and a Vote of the People."[17] Can you explain the circumstances surrounding this?

GADAMER: This was a signature that probably originated in the spring [of 1933] in Marburg, in a meeting in which we were publicly asked if anyone at all was against it, and nobody had the courage to say yes. Why? Because that would have meant emigration. This was how significant it was whether one signed onto this call. Gerhard Krüger und Werner Krauss also signed it. Krüger was a friend of mine, quite closely tied with Bultmann and the confessing church. Krauss was later a member of the Red Chapel.[18] I assume that the signatures of support for Hitler that were collected by acclamation were simply placed under this heading in the ad in November. I certainly know that I never saw this thing, initiated by Heidegger, that came out of Saxony.

WESTERNHAGEN: With this, we come to the second question: How did you who were not forced to leave survive? Accommodation? Disguise? And to you yourself, what about the protest of the National Socialist Teacher's Union against the professor title in 1935?

GADAMER: That was in 1934–1935.

WESTERNHAGEN: After that came your voluntary registration in that teachers camp. Why did you think you had to voluntarily register for this?[19]

GADAMER: Otherwise only people who were born with a silver spoon in their mouth got the professorships. I thought it over. How can I hold out against the opposition of the Party and at the same time not commit a breach of faith with my Jewish friends? I said, I will go voluntarily into one of these camps and see what happens. Perhaps it will help me. And it did help me. Not that I stated there that I was a supporter of the Nazis.

WESTERNHAGEN: How did it help you?

GADAMER: Through the influence of the leader of the camp. Our whole later careers depended on the fact that many people went into the Party and later were in leading positions who were absolutely honorable and reasonable people and who now used their influence in order to advance cultural politics in their sense of it. Freyer also belongs in this group.

WESTERNHAGEN: I would like to know a little more about classical philology as an area into which you claim you could retreat, as to an ivory tower. You depict Leipzig in this way in your autobiography. But wasn't the powerful school of Karl Reinhardt, Schadewaldt and Berve there? How could classical philology escape the ideological grip of the Nazis?

GADAMER: There's no doubt that Schadewaldt was influenced by Heidegger to become a Nazi, and likewise Berve, who, as an old Silesian nationalist and conservative, became a Nazi. But it is thanks to both of these people, especially Berve, that people like us were protected. Berve became rector in Leipzig and protected us. Countless times there were denunciations against me. I was ordered before the rector, who said: "We have been asked by the Gestapo why you did X . . . " I have told the story about "All asses are brown" in my autobiography. In such cases, Berve and others protected me and others.

WESTERNHAGEN: The Nazis tried to make all possible academic disciplines serviceable to them. That is a major trend that Berve, too, could not hinder.

GADAMER: Yes, but this we were able to sidestep. When I was suddenly called to Leipzig, the Ancestral Heritage Project approached me. And these sorts of things I declined.

WESTERNHAGEN: What did they want from you?

GADAMER: Oh, to cooperate on something to do with Plato. I declined.

WESTERNHAGEN: Did the Ancestral Heritage Project have to do with philosophy "am Hut"? Schilling—

GADAMER: Exactly. Schilling was the person who was also a student of mine.[20]

WESTERNHAGEN: What did he want?

GADAMER: At that time, the SS planned an elite cultural politics, so to speak, which is what that cockfight of the SS against Goebbels was all about. Krüger had not yet been called there, but Schilling was also his student. Schilling was an insignificant person who surely also had culture in mind, but of course as a subordinate working within the movement. Many collaborated in it and wrote respectable works. They were printed. But I did not work with them. I was already able to do this, if I may express it cynically, because, through a miracle of God, I had already received a professorship. So I was able to say, "Yes, but unfortunately I don't have any time."

WESTERNHAGEN: Now with regard to the influence of the Nazis on classical philology: There certainly were Nazi-ideologists or former conservatives also in this discipline.

GADAMER: Once again, remember that there were not just conservatives in this discipline. There were also highly liberal people; there were many who were closely associated with left-wing Jewish intellectuals. Look, it would be a long story if I tried to set forth how, during the Weimar Republic [prior to Hitler] an interest in the political dimensions of Plato developed. At that time this had nothing to do with the Nazis. Rather, interest in the political side of Plato at that time satisfied a need to put forward a model of a state because there was still interest in imagining a state [*Staatsgesinnung*]. For in the Weimar Republic there wasn't any.

WESTERNHAGEN: Yes, good; that is an answer.

GADAMER: And people like Schadewaldt were called to this cause.

WESTERNHAGEN: And then these lines of thinking were further developed in the Third Reich?

GADAMER: They were carried further by him, yes. But please not by Karl Reinhardt, not by Friedrich Klingner, not by me! For you to let us be abused in this way is certainly not necessary. Classical philology was indeed precisely an area into which people retreated. What I am saying is that there were only a few, a small fraction, who were working along these lines. But they were still in solidarity with us because what they were doing in the way of scholarship was still good scientific work. Richard Harder is for me an interesting example of this solidarity in relation to quality work in the discipline, even if one was a Nazi.[21]

WESTERNHAGEN: In your autobiography you make it appear as if in the Leipzig period nobody at all ever had anything to do with the

Party. What did the oppositional thinking look like that you had in mind in that book, that you could not express or could do so only among friends?

GADAMER: Everything that you think about the period today: What a tragedy it is that we have these demogogues and their unscrupulous band of followers governing us! And there was the Gestapo, whose omniscience we probably overestimated. That I admit. We all had a part in spreading the terror by overestimating the knowledge the Gestapo had. We believed they knew everything. I experienced that personally: my wife was brought before the People's Court of Justice on account of a remark she had made on the street. It was about a friend of Goerdeler; his daughter was a student of mine. We all were worried when Goerdeler blew his top.

WESTERNHAGEN: A side issue: Why did you put the word "emigrant" in quotation marks when you stated in your autobiography that Werner Jaeger went to the U.S. in 1936 as "emigrant"?[22]

GADAMER: It had no special meaning. He was "Jewish-connected" by marriage, but one did not know that. By that I simply meant he went voluntarily. Also, it was one of the countless cases at the beginning where we said to ourselves: 'Well, I'll be damned! What a decision and what courage!' I turned the question around to read: Why didn't they stay?

WESTERNHAGEN: They could not.

GADAMER: Either they were Jews or they were "Jewish-connected."

WESTERNHAGEN: Or politically out of favor.

GADAMER: Hold on a minute! This is where it gets more interesting.

WESTERNHAGEN: For instance, Aloys Wenzl, Paul Tillich.[23] The Frankfurt School people—

GADAMER: Among those who were then politically out of favor [and had to go] you have only named two doubtful names.

WESTERNHAGEN: Wenzl was SPD [*Sozialdemokratische Partei Deutschlands*].

GADAMER: That was not the basis.

WESTERNHAGEN: Why not?

GADAMER: Because if that had been so, then we would have lost a whole pile of Nazis.

WESTERNHAGEN: Well, he did not emigrate, but he was put out of his job.

GADAMER: Not on account of SPD, not at all. He must have done something else. Certainly it was not just on account of being a member of the SPD...

WESTERNHAGEN: Oh yes it was! On account of political unreliability, paragraph 4 of the Law for the Rebuilding of the Civil Service.

GADAMER: One could do that, of course. The Munich relationships I did not know. What about other cases? Who else had to go for other reasons?

WESTERNHAGEN: Those who were racially persecuted.

GADAMER: All that is granted.

WESTERNHAGEN: All granted?

GADAMER: That is indeed my thesis. I have always asked myself: why did we stay? Now I can explain to you the quotation marks on "emigrant." Is an emigrant someone who leaves voluntarily or is he forced to go? If he was only going because he was forced to do so, then like everybody else, I did not have to reflect on why we did not go. Then we could say, and I cite Mr. Kippenberg, the old editor for Insel publishers: *Et illud transit.*

WESTERNHAGEN: What does that mean?

GADAMER: "This too will pass." And Germany will remain. Indeed, in this way we stayed alive. Under this motto! This too will pass. These terrible episodes will one day be over, and it will at least be something that we are still around. I do not mean just personally; rather, this is something that the whole time taught us. It was well understood that, although I was not allowed to say from the podium, "I hold this, believe this, have written this," I was still allowed to hold seminars, even on Jewish authors, undisturbed. Nobody denounced this. Why? God yes, of course. Because the Nazis didn't give a damn what we did. Students, they could be dangerous because they would number in the thousands. But about the few professors, they didn't care a rap. These intellectuals, they thought, what did it matter what they had in their heads? This is what we were in their estimation! For this reason, I think your whole standpoint of questioning about the role of philosophy is . . . about this I can only say: No, the real Nazis had no interest in us at all.

WESTERNHAGEN: But there were certainly a large number of philosophers who philosophized in the sense of the Nazis. Bruno Bauch, Heimsoeth, Gehlen, Freyer—

GADAMER: There were a very few who spoke in this way from the podium. I always said that I would ten times rather have as a professor somebody who went into the Party in order to hold onto his position or to gain a position, and who then practices rational philosophy, than such people as Becker or Freyer, who were not in the Party but who spoke like Nazis.

WESTERNHAGEN: I find it hard to determine quantitatively what the relationships were.

GADAMER: You could determine it from their writings. If you look at my publications in the Third Reich, you will discover that after 1935 all I wrote was one single book. But now that is the way most of us conducted ourselves.

WESTERNHAGEN: I would like to talk about Theodor Litt. In a 1933 lecture he asked: How can the humanities serve the state and at the same time also serve truth? Litt is regarded as an example of inner emigration.[24]

GADAMER: Not a bad example. He was a very upright man.

WESTERNHAGEN: Would you also see yourself as a case of inner emigration?

GADAMER: We all were. That is nothing special. Of course we were.

WESTERNHAGEN: What about *"Der Kriegseinsatz der Geisteswissenschaften"*—"The Stake of the Humanities in the War"?

GADAMER: This was an initiative by university teachers in the humanities and social sciences who maintained that the financial support of the natural sciences was out of proportion.

WESTERNHAGEN: And the *DFG* [*Deutsche Forschungsgemeinschaft* (German Society for Research)] together with the Ministry of Education started work on volumes titled, "The Image of War in German Thought" and "The German Element in German Philosophy."

GADAMER: I did take part in one of those meetings. Rothacker was also there.

WESTERNHAGEN: Joachim Ritter[25] and Weinhandl,[26] too.

GADAMER: Joachim Ritter was much more of a Nazi at that time; he was a younger man.

WESTERNHAGEN: You write in one place that this project saved many lives. How are we to understand this? Was it because one acquired a deferment?

GADAMER: No, what I had in mind above all was the translator companies. It was [Wilhelm] Canaris we have to thank for this defense strategy that saved an infinite number of lives [of teachers in the humanities and social sciences]. The device was to invent translator companies, a service which protected people in the humanities from military service. They could learn Chinese, or whatever, so that after the final victory, when we conquer China, for instance, then we immediately have ready the right people to translate for us—a somewhat malicious example, but quite near reality.

WESTERNHAGEN: From the vantage point of today, it was an insertion of the humanities into the war effort. The articles and essays from the war volume, for example, were sent to the front as individual publications. This strengthened the people on the front in their effort.

GADAMER: But read *The Heritage of Antiquity* for yourself. These are the two volumes that we as classical philologists did. They are still on the market today unchanged. Popitz[27] took charge of the matter. For this reason it went well. You are right, of course, that these projects all contributed to the war effort, even philosophy, but once again one saw what would happen to those who did not cooperate. I mean the pressure was intense. I was just a little more clever in choosing one way rather than the other. I must say, I do not claim any moral qualities for this, only political. I was more clever. Others, because they could not get through it otherwise, had to make concessions. I did not have to do that. My cleverness [*Geschicktheit*] consisted in taking seriously as colleagues those who were Nazis but who were also at the same time genuine, rational scholars; avoiding, of course, political conversation. That is what carried me along. That's how I got to Leipzig.

WESTERNHAGEN: On this point, please answer my final question: How does one in the midst of the Third Reich become a professor in Leipzig?

GADAMER: Exactly in the way I have described. I would like to add one thing. Yes, I was politically more clever than others, but I also had a moral motive: Not to lose the confidence of my Jewish friends. On the whole, this feeling of solidarity that I experienced enabled me to hold out during this time. Without that, this account sounds much too pragmatic. There was a moral background also present.

Bibliography

Translator's note: The original bibliography supplied the publication data for works cited parenthetically in the text and endnotes simply by giving the author's last name, initials, and year of publication. Although the German publishers' names were omitted in Westernhagen's German bibliography, as was the custom, these have been added as is customary with American bibliographical protocol. Also, the original bibliography did not give the inclusive page numbers of articles in journals or books. These have been added where possible. Finally, the English translations have also been added where available. Any other additional information appears in brackets.

Asmus, W. *Richard Kroner (1884–1974): Ein Philosoph und Pädagoge unter dem Schatten Hitlers.* Frankfurt/M., Bern, New York: Peter Lang, 1990.

Berve, H., ed. *Das Neue Bild der Antike* (2 vols.). Leipzig: Koehler und Amelang, 1942.

Boberach, H., ed. *Meldungen aus dem Reich: Die geheimen Lageberichte des Sicherheitsdienstes der SS 1938–1945.* Neuwied: Luchterhand, 1965.

Cassirer, T. *Mein Leben mit Ernst Cassirer.* Hildesheim: Gerstenberg, 1981.

Dahms, H. J. "Aufstieg und Ende der Lebensphilosophie: Das Philosophische Seminar der Universität Göttingen zwischen 1917 und 1950." In H. Becker et al. ed., *Die Universität Göttingen unter dem Nationalsozialismus.* Munich: GK Saur, 1987 (169–99).

Farías, V. *Heidegger und der Nationalsozialismus.* Frankfurt/M.: S. Fischer, 1989. Enhanced version in English: *Heidegger and Nazism.* Translated from the French original text of 1987 by Paul Burrell, with additions from the German edition. Philadelphia: Temple University Press, 1989.

Griederich, Th. "Theodor Litts Warnung vor 'allzu direkten Methoden.'" In Haug (1989), see below, pp. 99–125.

Gadamer, H.-G. *Philosophische Lehrjahre: Eine Rückschau.* Frankfurt: Klostermann, 1977a. English: *Philosophical Apprenticeships.* Translated by Robert R. Sullivan. Cambridge: The MIT University Press, 1985.

Gadamer, H.-G. "Selbstdarstellung." In L. J. Pongratz, ed., *Philosophie in Selbstdarstellungen* (vol. 3). Hamburg: Meiner, 1977b. An English translation of this essay can be found in *Philosophical Apprenticeships,* ibid., pp. 177–93, and it also constitutes the first part of "Reflections on a Philosophical Journey," in Lewis E. Hahn ed., *The Philosophy of Hans-Georg Gadamer* (La Salle, Ill.: Open Court Press, 1997), pp. 3–18.

Goldschmidt, U. K. "Wilamowitz and the Georgekreis: New Documents." In W. M. Calder et al. ed., *Wilamowitz nach 50 Jahren.* Darmstadt: Wissenschaftliche Buchgesellschaft, 1985 (583–612).

Haug, Wolfgang Fritz. *Die Faschisierung des bürgerlichen Subjekts: Die Ideologie der gesunden Normalität und die Ausrottungspolitiken in deutschen Faschismus.* West Berlin: Argument-Verlag, 1986.

Haug, Wolfgang Fritz, ed. *Deutsche Philosophen 1933.* West Berlin: Argument-Verlag, 1989. Vol. 3 of the series "Ideologische Mächte im deutschen Faschismus."

Henckmann, W. "Philosophie an der Universität München 1933–1945." In *Widerspruch—Münchner Zeitschrift für Philosophie,* vol. 13 (1987), page numbers not available.

Klinger, G. "Freiheit als 'freiwillige Aufgabe der Freiheit': Arnold Gehlens Umbau des deutschen Idealismus." In Haug (1989), pp. 188–218.

Leske, M. *Philosophen im Dritten Reich. Studie zu Hochschul- und Philosophiebetrieb im faschistischen Deutschland.* Berlin/DDR: Dietz, 1990.

Loseman, V. *Nationalsozialismus und Antike: Studien zur Entwicklung des Faches Alte Geschichte 1933–1945.* Hamburg: Hoffmann und Campe, 1977.

Löwith, K. *Mein Leben in Deutschland vor und nach 1933: Ein Bericht.* Stuttgart: Metzler, 1986. English: *My Life in Germany before and after 1933: A Report.* Urbana: University of Illinois Press, 1994.

Meran, Josef. "Die Lehrer am Philosophischen Seminar der Hamburger Universität während der Zeit des Nationalsozialismus." In Eckart Krause, Ludwig Huber, and Holger Fischer, ed., *Hochschulalltag im Dritten Reich. Die Hamburger Universität 1933 bis 1945.* West-Berlin: Reimer, 1990 [1991]. II: 459–82.

Muller, J. Z. *The Other God That Failed: Hans Freyer and the Deradicalization of German Conservatism.* Princeton, N.J.: Princeton University Press, 1987.

Poliakov, L. and J. Wulf, ed. *Das Dritte Reich und seine Denker.* West Berlin: Arani, 1959. [Subsequently republished several times.]

Rügemer, W. *Philosophische Anthropologie und Epochenkrise: Studie über den Zusammenhang von allg. Krise des Kapitalismus und die anthropologischen Grundlegung der Philosophy am Beispiel Arnold Gehlens.* Köln: Pahl-Rugenstein, 1979.

Schelsky, H. *Rückblicke eines "Anti-Soziologen."* Opladen: Westdeutscher Verlag, 1981.

Schneider, U. "Widerstand und Verfolgung an der Marburger Universität 1933–1945." In Dieter Kramer und Christina Janja, eds., *Universität und demokratische Bewegung: ein Lesebuch zur 450-Jahrfeier der Philipps-Universität.* Marburg: Verlag Arbeiterbewegung und Gesellschaftswissen, 1977 (219–56).

Weber, Th., 1989a. "Arbeit am Imaginären des Deutschen: Erich Rothackers Ideen für eine NS-Kulturpolitik." In Haug (1989), pp. 125–58.

Weber, Th., 1989b. "Joachim Ritter und die 'metaphysische Wendung.'" In Haug (1989), pp. 219–43.

[Wistrich, Robert S. *Der antisemitische Wahn: von Hitler bis zum Heiligen Krieg gegen Israel.* Munich: M. Hueber, 1987. Cited parenthetically by Westernhagen but accidentally omitted from the bibliography.]

BIBLIOGRAPHICAL APPENDIX A

TRANSLATIONS OF *HERMENEUTIK-*

ÄSTHETIK-PRAKTISCHE

PHILOSOPHIE: HANS-GEORG

GADAMER IM GESPRÄCH

German original: *Hermeneutik-Ästhetik-Praktische Philosophie: Hans-Georg Gadamer im Gespräch.* Conversations with and edited by Carsten Dutt. Heidelberg: Universitätsverlag Carl Winter, 1993. Second edition, bibliographically updated, 1995, third edition, 2000.

Japanese: *Gâdamâ to no Taiwa: Kaishakugaku, Bigadu, Jissentetsugaku* (Poiêsisu-Sôshô). Translated by Etsuro Makita. Tokyo: Mirai-sha, 1995.

Italian: *Dialogando con Gadamer: Ermeneutica, estetica, filosofia pratica.* Translated by Andrea Pinotti. Milan: Raffaello Cortina, 1995.

Spanish: *En conversación con Hans-Georg Gadamer: Hermenéutica, Estética, Filosofía práctica.* Ed. Carsten Dutt. Introduced and translated by Teresa Rocha Barco. Madrid: Tecnos, 1998.

French: *Herméneutique, esthétique, philosophie pratique: dialogue avec Hans-Georg Gadamer.* By Carsten Dutt. Translation of the second edition by Donald Ipperciel. Saint Lawrence, Canada: Fides, 1998.

BIBLIOGRAPHICAL APPENDIX B

ENGLISH-LANGUAGE BOOKS

BY AND ABOUT GADAMER

Books by Gadamer in English (in order of English publication)

Truth and Method. Translated by G. Barden and J. Cumming. N.Y.: Sheed and Ward, 1976. Translation revised for second edition in 1989 by Joel Weinsheimer and Donald G. Marshall. New York: Crossroad. 579 pp., including all supplements. German title and subtitle: *Wahrheit und Methode: Grundzüge einer philosophischen Hermeneutik.* First edition 1960, 503 pp., fifth and sixth editions, 1986. Its location in *Gesammelte Werke* is 1 (1986): 1–494. The supplements and appendices from earlier editions appear in volume 2 (1986). The first two volumes together carry the title *Hermeneutik I and II.*

Hegel's Dialectic: Five Hermeneutical Studies. Translated by P. C. Smith. New Haven: Yale University Press, 1976. German first edition, 1971.

Reason in the Age of Science. Translated by Frederick G. Lawrence. Cambridge, Mass.: MIT Press, 1981. German first edition, 1976.

Philosophical Apprenticeships. Translated by Robert R. Sullivan. Cambridge, Mass.: MIT Press, 1985. Gadamer's autobiography, with recollections of famous scholars. German first edition, 1977.

Lectures on Philosophical Hermeneutics. Pretoria: Universiteit van Pretoria, 1982.

The Idea of the Good in Platonic-Aristotelian Philosophy. Translated and introduced by P. Christopher Smith. New Haven: Yale University Press, 1986. German first edition, 1978.

The Relevance of the Beautiful and Other Essays. Edited by R. Bernasconi, translated by Nick Walker. Cambridge: Cambridge University Press, 1986. The title essay, *Die Aktualität des Schönen: Kunst als Spiel, Symbol und Fest,* was published in German as a booklet in 1977. *RB* contains ten other essays, mostly from two volumes in the four-volume set of Gadamer's *Kleine Schriften,* vol. 2: *Interpretationen* (Tübingen: Mohr, 1967) and 4: *Variationen* (Tübingen: Mohr, 1977).

Plato's Dialectical Ethics: Phenomenological Interpretations Relating to the Philebus. Translated by R. M. Wallace. New Haven: Yale University Press, 1991. From the third edition, 1983; first edition, 1931.

Heidegger's Ways. Translated by John W. Stanley and introduced by Dennis J. Schmidt. Albany: State University of New York Press, 1994. German first edition, 1983.

The Enigma of Health: The Art of Healing in a Scientific Age. Translated by Jason Geiger and Nick Walker. Cambridge, U.K.: Polity Press, 1995, paper, 1996. Stanford, Calif.: Stanford University Press, 1996. German first edition, 1993.

Gadamer on Celan: Who Am I and Who Are You? and Other Essays. Translated and edited by Richard Heinemann and Bruce Krajewski, with an introduction by Gerald L. Bruns. Albany: State University of New York Press, 1997. First German edition of title essay, 1973.

The Beginning of Philosophy. Translated by Rod Coltman. New York: Continuum, 1998. German first edition, 1997.

Praise of Theory: Speeches and Essays. Translated by Chris Dawson. New Haven: Yale University Press, 1998. German first edition, 1983.

The Beginning of Knowledge. By Rod Coltman. Translation of *Der Anfang des Wissens.* First edition, Stuttgart: Reclam, 1999. New York: Continuum, 2002. A companion series of lectures to *The Beginning of Philosophy,* also delivered in Italy, published there, and translated back into German.

Books Collecting and Translating Articles by Gadamer
(in order of English publication)

Philosophical Hermeneutics. Translated by David E. Linge. Berkeley: University of California Press, 1976. Important collection of Gadamer's shorter writings.

The Relevance of the Beautiful and Other Essays. Edited by R. Bernasconi, translated by Nick Walker. Cambridge: Cambridge University Press, 1986. While the title essay, *Die Aktualität des Schönen: Kunst als Spiel, Symbol und Fest,* was published in German in book form in 1977, the volume collects and translates ten other essays, mostly from volumes 2 and 4 in the four-volume set of Gadamer's *Kleine Schriften*: vol. 2: *Interpretationen* (Tübingen: Mohr, 1967) and 4: *Variationen* (Tübingen: Mohr, 1977).

Dialogue and Dialectic: Eight Hermeneutical Studies on Plato. Translated and with an introduction by P. Christopher Smith. New Haven: Yale University Press, 1980. A selection of Gadamer's most important essays on Plato.

Dialogue and Deconstruction: The Gadamer–Derrida Encounter. Translated and edited by Diane P. Michelfelder and Richard E. Palmer. Albany: State University of New York, 1989. Includes "Text and Interpretation" and Gadamer's four other essays on deconstruction, plus commentary by scholars. His one later essay on deconstruction,"Hermeneutik auf die Spur," in *GW* 10 (1995): 148–74, remains untranslated.

Hans-Georg Gadamer on Education, Poetry, and History: Applied Hermeneutics. Edited by Dieter Misgeld and Graeme Nicholson, translated by Lawrence K. Schmidt and Monika Reuss. Albany: State University of New York Press, 1992. Contains four interviews with Gadamer on various topics, plus essays in the areas mentioned in the title.

Literature and Philosophy in Dialogue: Essays in German Literary Theory by Hans-Georg Gadamer. Translated by Robert H. Paslick. Albany: State University of New York Press, 1994. Many essays from Gadamer's *Poetica*, 1977 and 1990.

Hermeneutics, Religion, and Ethics. Translated by J. Weinsheimer. New Haven: Yale University Press, 1999.

A Gadamer Reader. Translated and edited by Richard E. Palmer. Evanston: Northwestern University Press, 2002. A translation of the *Gadamer Lesebuch*, edited by Jean Grondin. Tübingen: Mohr Siebeck, 1997.

English-Language Books About Gadamer or Philosophical Hermeneutics
(in alphabetical order)
Books by Individual Authors

(Translator's note: Masters and Ph.D. theses in English on hermeneutics and Gadamer's thought number well over a hundred, so these had to be excluded from this list, even though many titles looked very interesting. For help on how to find these see Appendix C.)

Alejandro, Roberto. *Hermeneutics, Citizenship, and the Public Sphere.* Albany: State University of New York Press, 1993.

Bleicher, Josef. *Contemporary Hermeneutics: Hermeneutics as Method, Philosophy and Critique.* London: Routledge and Kegan Paul, 1980. 288 pp., bib. 272–80. Second edition, 1990.

The Cambridge Companion to Gadamer. Edited by Robert Dostal. Cambridge: Cambridge University Press, 2001. Contains an extensive bibliography of Gadamer's writings translated into English and of works in English about Gadamer and philosophical hermeneutics.

Cameron, Scott. *On Gadamer and Habermas.* Book in progress.

Carr, Thomas K. *Newman and Gadamer: Toward a Hermeneutics of Religious Knowledge.* Atlanta, Ga.: Scholars Press, 1996.

Coltman, Rod. *The Language of Hermeneutics: Gadamer and Heidegger in Dialogue.* Albany: State University of New York Press, 1998.

Feminist Interpretations of Gadamer. Edited by Lorraine Code. State College: Pennsylvania State University Press, 2002.

Foster, Matthew Robert. *Gadamer and Practical Philosophy: The Hermeneutics of Moral Confidence.* Atlanta, Ga.: Scholars Press, 1991.

Gallagher, Shaun. *Hermeneutics and Education.* Albany: State University of New York Press, 1992.

Grondin, Jean. *Introduction to Gadamer.* London: Acumen Publisher, 2002. A translation of his *Einführing zu Gadamer.* Stuttgart: Uni-TB, 2000.

Grondin, Jean. *Introduction to Philosophical Hermeneutics.* New Haven: Yale University Press, 1995.

Grondin, Jean. *Sources of Hermeneutics.* Albany: State University of New York Press, 1996.

How, Alan. *The Gadamer–Habermas Debate and the Nature of the Social: Back to Bedrock.* Brookfield, Vt.: Avebury, 1995.

Howard, Roy J. *Three Faces of Hermeneutics: An Introduction to Current Theories of Understanding.* Berkeley: University of California Press, 1982. 182 pp., bib. 177–84.

Hoy, David Couzens. *The Critical Circle: Literature, History, and Philosophical Hermeneutics.* Berkeley: University of California Press, 1978.

Johnson, Patricia A. *On Gadamer.* Belmont, Calif.: Wadsworth/Thomson Learning, 2000.

Kögler, Hans Herbert. *The Power of Dialogue: Critical Hermeneutics after Gadamer and Foucault.* Cambridge, Mass.: MIT Press, 1996.

Kush, Martin. *Language as Calculus vs. Language as Universal Medium: A Study of Husserl, Heidegger, and Gadamer.* Dordrecht: Kluwer Academic Pubs., 1989. 362 pp., bib. 315–42.

Lawler, Justus George. *The 1994 Annual of Hermeneutics and Social Concern.* New York: Continuum, 1994.

Madison, Gary B. *The Hermeneutics of Postmodernity: Figures and Themes.* Bloomington: Indiana University Press, 1988. 206 pp., bib. refs.

Palmer, Richard E. *Hermeneutics: Interpretation Theory in Schleiermacher, Dilthey,*

Heidegger, and Gadamer. Evanston: Northwestern University Press, 1969. 282 pp., bib. 254–74.

Ricoeur, Paul. *Hermeneutics and the Human Sciences.* Translated by John B. Thompson. New York: Cambridge University Press, 1981. 314 pp., bib. 306–08.

Risser, James. *Hermeneutics and the Voice of the Other: Re-reading Gadamer's Philosophical Hermeneutics.* Albany: State University of New York Press, 1997.

Roberts, David. *Reconstructing Theory: Gadamer, Habermas, Luhmann.* Melbourne University Press, 1995.

Scheibler, Ingrid. *Gadamer: Between Heidegger and Habermas.* Lanham, Md.: Rowman and Littlefield, 2000.

Schmidt, Lawrence K. *The Epistemology of Hans-Georg Gadamer.* New York: Peter Lang, 1985. Second edition, 1987.

Smith, P. Christopher. *Hermeneutics and Human Finitude: Toward a Theory of Ethical Understanding.* New York: Fordham University Press, 1991.

Smith, P. Christopher. *The Hermeneutics of Original Argument: Demonstration, Dialectic, Rhetoric.* Evanston: Northwestern University Press, 1998.

Sullivan, Robert. *Political Hermeneutics: The Early Thinking of Hans-Georg Gadamer.* University Park: Pennsylvania State University Press, 1990.

Teigas, Demetrius. *Knowledge and Hermeneutic Understanding: A Study of the Habermas–Gadamer Debate.* Bucknell University Press, 1995.

Vattimo, Gianni. *Beyond Interpretation: The Meaning of Hermeneutics for Philosophy.* Stanford, Calif.: Stanford University Press, 1997.

Wachterhauser, Brice. *Beyond Being: Gadamer's Post-Platonic Hermeneutic Ontology.* Evanston: Northwestern University Press, 1999.

Warnke, Georgia. *Gadamer: Hermeneutics, Tradition and Reason.* Stanford, Calif.: Stanford University Press, 1987.

Weinsheimer, Joel C. *Gadamer's Hermeneutics: A Reading of "Truth and Method."* New Haven: Yale University Press, 1985.

Weinsheimer, Joel C. *Philosophical Hermeneutics and Literary Theory.* New Haven: Yale University Press, 1991.

Collections of Articles on Gadamer or Hermeneutics

Dialogue and Deconstruction: The Gadamer–Derrida Encounter. Edited and translated by Diane P. Michel-felder and Richard E. Palmer, with an introduction. Albany: State University of New York Press, 1989. 316 pp., bib. 284–91, bib. refs. 295–316. Brief question-and-answer encounter at a conference on text and interpretation in Paris, April 1981. A dozen expert essays, plus four by Gadamer, interpret the encounter.

Festivals of Interpretation: Essays on Hans-Georg Gadamer's Work. Edited by Kathleen Wright. Albany: State University of New York Press, 1990. 248 pp., footnotes, but no bib.

Gadamer and Hermeneutics. Edited by Hugh J. Silverman. New York: Routledge, 1991. 309 pp., bib. of books in English by Hélène Volat-Shapiro, 311–27.

Hermeneutical Inquiry. Edited by D. E. Klemm. Vol 1: *The Interpretation of Texts.* 285 pp. Vol. 2: *The Interpretation of Existence.* 323 pp. Atlanta: Scholars Press, 1986. Bib. in vol. 2: 273–323. An anthology of texts by Schleiermacher, Dilthey, Heidegger, Gadamer, Bultmann, Tillich, etc. Primarily for theological students.

Hermeneutics and Modern Philosophy. Edited by Brice Wachterhauser. Albany: State University of New York Press, 1986. 506 pp., bib. 487–502.

Hermeneutics and Praxis. Edited by Robert Hollinger. Notre Dame, Ind.: University of Notre Dame Press, 1985. 296 pp., no bib.

Hermeneutics and Truth. Edited by Brice R. Wachterhauser. Albany: State Univesity of New York Press, 1994. 255 pp., bib. 229–55.

Hermeneutics: Questions and Prospects. Edited by Gary Shapiro and Alan Sica. Amherst: University of Massachusetts Press, 1984. 307 pp., bib. 292–307.

The Hermeneutic Tradition: From Ast to Ricoeur. Edited by Gayle Ormiston and Alan Schrift. Albany: State University of New York Press, 1989. 380 pp., bib. 335–65.

Interrogating the Tradition: Hermeneutics and the History of Philosophy. Edited by Charles E. Scott and John Sallis. Albany: State University of New York Press, 2000. 299 pp., no bib.

Language and Linguisticality in Gadamer's Hermeneutics. Edited by Lawrence K. Schmidt. Lanham, Md.: Lexington Books, 2000.

The Philosophy of Hans-Georg Gadamer. Edited by Lewis E. Hahn. Library of Living Philosophers Series, vol. 24. Chicago and LaSalle, Ill.: Open Court, 1997. 602 pp. A major resource and reference work on Gadamer containing a sixty-page autobiographical sketch, a fifty-five-page bibliography, plus twenty-nine critical essays and Gadamer's reply to each of them.

Rhetoric and Hermeneutics in Our Time: A Reader. Edited by Walter Jost and Michael J. Hyde. New Haven: Yale University Press, 1997. Contains translations of two of Gadamer's essays on rhetoric. Relates hermeneutics to rhetoric.

Special Gadamer issues of journals: *Continental Philosophy Review,* vol. 33, 2000. *Revue internationale de philosophie,* no. 3, 2000.

The Specter of Relativism: Truth, Dialogue and Phronesis in Philosophical Hermeneutics. Edited by Lawrence K. Schmidt. Evanston, Ill.: Northwestern University Press, 1995. 295 pp., bib. 271–91.

BIBLIOGRAPHICAL APPENDIX C

HOW TO FIND THESES,
ARTICLES, AND OTHER WRITINGS
BY AND ABOUT GADAMER

Since the lists in the previous appendices are only of books, not articles (space here would not allow their inclusion), and not even the hundreds of masters and doctoral theses, this final appendix will offer a few hints to those seeking articles and other writings by or about Gadamer in English and other languages.

First, the definitive bibliographical reference work on Gadamer's writings is the *Gadamer-Bibliographie (1922–1994)*, 349 pages, by Etsuro Makita. Published in German by Peter Lang (New York, Paris, Frankfurt, Vienna) in 1995, it is an indispensable reference for every serious Gadamer scholar and library. Well-indexed, it lists in chronological order each book, article, book review, published letter, or interview by Gadamer—and all the available translations that Makita was able to unearth, and he found astonishingly many! But he could not include books and articles *about* Gadamer (i.e., secondary sources). In chronological order Makita lists the original German publication of each book, article, review, or interview, then he attempts to list translations of it in all languages—Polish, Czech, Italian, French, Spanish, Finnish, Japanese, etc., and of course English. For instance, in addition to English, twelve translations of *Truth and Method* are listed. Makita's bibliography is helping Gadamer scholars all over the world. Although the explanatory and descriptive material is in German, the book can be used by non-German-speakers with the help of a basic German dictionary. A little logic decodes the classifications—books are listed first in chronological order under B (*Bücher*), followed by articles under A (*Aufsätze*), shorter writings and interviews under K (for *kleine*), and reviews under R. German words that are repeatedly used, like *herausgegeben von* (edited by), can be picked up quickly by the beginning user. Etsuro Makita, a professor of philosophy at Science University of Tokyo, has continued to update his Gadamer bibliography both with earlier works he overlooked and with writings that have been published since 1994. The updates may be accessed on his Gadamer Web site in German: www.ms.kuki.sut.ac.jp/ KMSLab/makita/neuers.html. He appreciates receiving copies of Gadamer writings that he may have omitted.

For a shorter and more selective bibliography of the major articles and books by Gadamer published in German and English but not in other languages, see "Hans-Georg Gadamer's Writings 1922–1996" in *The Philosophy of Hans-Georg Gadamer*, edited by Lewis E. Hahn, volume 24 in the "Library of Living Philosophers" series (Chicago and LaSalle, Ill.: Open Court, 1997): 555–602. Compiled by the present author, this list is based on Makita's comprehensive bibliography, with the addition of two pages listing honors Gadamer has received, a page or two of secondary books about Gadamer, plus a list of more than a hundred radio and television interviews, some of which were also in Makita's bibliography. The honors list ten memberships in scholarly "academies of arts and sciences" from all over the world (Boston, Rome, Athens, Budapest, London, Brussels, Leipzig, and others), twelve major prizes he received, including the highest prize that can be offered in Germany in any discipline (the Reuchlin prize), and seven honorary doctorates from universities all over the world. To this list can be added another honorary doctorate—from the University of Breslau (now Wroclaw, Poland) in 1998. The radio and television interviews that are listed are unfortunately almost exclusively from Germany, with a couple from Italy, so of course the many such broadcasts from the United States and around the world were left out. Still, this list is the first such publication of these interviews in German, which is valuable because scholars can obtain audio and video copies of them from the archives listed in the bibliography.

A twenty-seven-page bibliography in English, "Gadamer and Hermeneutics," was compiled by Hélène Volat-Shapiro in the collection of articles *Gadamer and Hermeneutics*, edited and introduced by Hugh J. Silverman (London and New York: Routledge, 1991), pp. 311–27. Unlike the list of books offered in these appendices, pp. 318–27 of this bibliography list both books and articles on Gadamer in English. And in 1998 a sixty-four-page bibliography *Hans-Georg Gadamer: A Bibliography* was published by Joan Nordquist (Santa Cruz: Reference and Research Services, 1998).

In addition, Robert Dostal has compiled an excellent recent bibliography of both articles in English by and about Gadamer and philosophical hermeneutics in his *Cambridge Companion to Gadamer* (Cambridge: Cambridge University Press, fall 2001 or 2002). The bibliography also lists books by Gadamer in German not contained in his collected works, including *Hermeneutische Entwürfe* (Tübingen: Mohr Siebeck, 2000), essentially an additional, eleventh volume of the collected works.

It is also helpful to know that volume 10 of the *Gesammelte Werke* lists the tables of contents of all ten volumes (all articles and books important enough to be included) and offers alphabetical indices of translated writings that are available in English, French, and Italian translations (pp. 472–79). Of particular value for readers of Gadamer in English is a list of 110 of Gadamer's essays in English on pp. 472–76. Published in 1995, however, the information in volume 10 is already dated by the considerable number of translations that have recently appeared. (For these consult the Makita Web site discussed above, which also contains some secondary sources.)

Finally, articles and dissertations about Gadamer can be located on the Internet and usually obtained at a reasonable price. In order to use the more specialized search engines—such as those available through OCLC (Online Cataloging Library Consortium)—a special library access code and password are needed. This means you probably will not be able to access it on your home computer and will instead have to go to a public or university library. Assuming you have library access to academic search engines, you can use First Search on the OCLC, if available, and the search engine called "World Cat" (World Catalog) to find the titles of books and masters and doctoral theses on Gadamer and hermeneutics in the on-line university card catalogs and in the Library of Congress. For hundreds of articles by and about Gadamer, try "Wilson Select" search engine and other specialized search engines available on OCLC First Search. Also, new search engines, such as EBSCO, are available. Many articles can be printed directly from a Web site (sometimes for no charge); other entries give only an abstract. A valuable new Internet resource is the Northern Lights search engine (www. northernlights.com). When I entered "Gadamer" in the search engine, it generated over 11,000 entries! The text of whole articles may be downloaded for a fee. Once you have the bibliographical data of a master's or doctoral dissertation on Gadamer or hermeneutics, you can often obtain it through interlibrary loan, or you can usually order a reasonably priced copy from University of Michigan Microfilms. So in your local library you can now access not only its own holdings, but books and articles from all over the world, although access to articles in German is much more limited. Welcome to the brave new world of Internet specialized search engines!

NOTES

Introduction

1. The interaction with Habermas resulted in the widely discussed book *Hermeneutik und Ideologiekritik* [*Hermeneutics and the Critique of Ideology*] (Frankfurt: Suhrkamp, 1971). Gadamer's contribution to the debate, "Rhetorik, Hermeneutik und Ideologiekritik," was quickly translated as "On the Scope and Function of Hermeneutical Reflection" in *Continuum* 7 (1970): 77–95 and later appeared in the Gadamer collection of essays *Philosophical Hermeneutics*, translated and edited by David E. Linge (Berkeley: University of California Press, 1976): 18–43, and as "Rhetoric, Hermeneutics, and Ideology-Critique" in *Rhetoric and Hermeneutics in Our Time: A Reader*, ed. Walter Jost and Michael J. Hyde (Yale University Press, 1997), 313–34. It was clearly a mistake for the translator to change the title, as many people thought this essay had remained untranslated.

2. Gadamer's presentation at that debate, "Le Défi Herméneutique," and Derrida's brief response, "Bonnes Volontés de Puissance," and Gadamer's reply appeared in the *Revue internationale de philosophie* 38, no. 151 (1984): 333–40, 343–45. A translation of the papers presented by Gadamer and Derrida at the symposium with additional essays on deconstruction by Gadamer and by

scholars critiquing the encounter appeared in *Dialogue and Deconstruction: The Gadamer–Derrida Encounter,* translated and edited by Diane P. Michelfelder and Richard E. Palmer (Albany: State University of New York Press, 1989).

3. Because Gadamer spent the first seventeen years of his life in Breslau, Germany (now Wroclaw, Poland), this is sometimes erroneously given as his birthplace. Gadamer's father, a university professor of pharmacological science at Marburg, was called to Breslau in 1901 and remained there until 1918, when he was called back to Marburg University. He died in 1927.

4. *Plato's Dialectical Ethics: Phenomenological Interpretations Relating to the Philebus.* Translated by R. M. Wallace (Yale University Press, 1991). Originally published in German in 1931, the German text can be found in *GW* [*Gesammelte Werke*] 5 (1987): 3–163.

5. Essays in tribute to many of these persons, including Paul Natorp, Max Scheler, Hans Lipps, Richard Benz, Karl Jaspers, Gerhard Krüger, and Karl Löwith, are recorded in his 1977 autobiographical memoir *Philosophische Lehrjahre: Eine Rückschau* (Frankfurt: Klostermann, 1977). Its English translation, *Philosophical Apprenticeships,* is by Robert R. Sullivan (Cambridge: MIT Press, 1985). A number of the essays in this volume were selected by Gadamer for inclusion in the last part of the final volume of his *GW* 10 (1995): 375–403. These stormy but exciting times for Gadamer are chronicled by his biographer, Jean Grondin, in a chapter titled "Marburger Dämonen," in *Hans-Georg Gadamer: Eine Biographie* (Tübingen: Mohr Siebeck, 1999), 80–107.

6. Richard Kroner in Kiel and Erich Frank in Marburg. See pp. 378–79 in the Grondin biography cited above. For a list of Gadamer's close Jewish friends, see Grondin, p. 148.

7. Grondin, p. 380 (January 1 entry).

8. Gadamer's interview with Dörte von Westernhagen, "Die wirklichen Nazis hatten doch überhaupt kein Interesse an uns" ["the real Nazis had no interest in us at all"], in *Das Argument* 182 (1990): 543–555, translated here, makes this clear. See also the interviews in *Hans-Georg Gadamer on Education, Poetry, and History* (1992), the last of which discusses his experiences with the Nazis. A recent book by Teresa Orozco, *Platonische Gewalt: Gadamers Politische Hermeneutik in der NS-Zeit* (Hamburg: Argument Verlag, 1995), tries to link Gadamer with the Nazis because he wrote about Plato during this period and lectured in France on Herder to French prisoners of war. Since Gadamer specialized in Plato long before the Hitler era, and had no association with the National Socialist Party, this argument seems far-fetched and unfair. The invitation to speak in France came from an old friend from his Marburg years. The book was negatively reviewed in the *Franffurter Allgemeine Zeituung* as totally failing to make its case. See "Mit Platon in den Führerstaat? Teresa Orozcos

Analyse von Gadamers Wirken unter dem Nationalsozialismus überzeugt nicht." *FAZ* Dec. 4, 1995 (http://afaz.gbi.de/cgi-bin/gbiwww). For my reply to an attack on Gadamer by Richard Wolin in the *New Republic* (May 15, 2000) based on Orozco's book, see my "Richard Wolin on Gadamer: Methodical Untruth" in *International Journal for Philosophical Studies* (forthcoming in late 2001 or 2002).

9. However, Grondin, in his Gadamer biography, p. 379, traces the origins of *TM* [*Truth and Method*] back to the 1936 summer course in Marburg, "Kunst und Geschichte (Einleitung in die Geisteswissenschaften)" saying that it laid the conceptual foundations for *TM*.

10. See Gadamer's reply in his "Rhetoric, Hermeneutics, and Ideology-Critique" in *Rhetoric and Hermeneutics in Our Time: A Reader*, edited by Walter Jost and Michael J. Hyde (Yale University Press, 1997), pp. 322–24, article pp. 313–34.

11. See Emilio Betti's pamphlet *Die Hermeneutik als allgemeine Methodik der Geisteswissenschaften* (Tübingen: J. C. B. Mohr, 1962), 62 pp., as well as his own translation of his 1955 masterwork from Italian into German as *Allgemeine Auslegungslehre als Methodik der Geisteswissenschaften* (Tübingen: J. C. B. Mohr, 1967), 771 pp. Also see the appendix to E. D. Hirsch, Jr., *Validity in Interpretation* (Yale University Press, 1967), which charges Gadamer with equating meaning with significance.

12. See *The Later Heidegger and Theology* and *The New Hermeneutic*, both edited by James M. Robinson and John B. Cobb, Jr. (New York: Harper & Row, 1963, 1964).

13. William Richardson, *Martin Heidegger: Through Phenomenology to Thought* (The Hague: Nijhoff, 1964). Richardson was a founding member of the Heidegger Circle in 1966, and already in the mid-sixties also the Society for Phenomenology and Existential Philosophy, which have both since met annually.

14. See the "Chronik" of Gadamer's life in Grondin, pp. 372–89. The period after 1968 is covered on pp. 386–89.

15. For a complete list of Gadamer's books in English, along with full publication information, see the second bibliographical appendix to this volume.

16. See my review of research, "Hermeneutics [1966–1978]," in *Contemporary Philosophy: A New Survey*, edited by Guttorm Fløistad, vol. 2: *Philosophy of Science* (Dordrecht: Nijhoff, 1981), pp. 453–505, esp. 479 ff. In an unpublished paper, "The Relevance of Hermeneutics," presented at Southern Illinois University, Carbondale, in April 1999, I discussed thirty-six areas and disciplines to which philosophical hermeneutics is relevant. The full text of this presentation is available on my Web site: www.mac.edu/~rpalmer/relevance.html.

17. See Etsuro Makita, *Gadamer-Bibliographie: 1922–1994* (Frankfurt: Peter

Lang, 1994), pp. 52–55. Updated annually on his Web site: www.ms.kuki.sut
.ac.jp/KMSLab/makita/neuers.html.

18. Ibid.

19. See *The Philosophy of Hans-Georg Gadamer*, ed. Lewis E. Hahn (LaSalle,
Ill.: Open Court Press, 1997), pp. 556–57, for a listing.

20. The encounter with Derrida is documented in *Dialogue and Deconstruction: The Gadamer-Derrida Encounter*. For Derrida's reference to it as a non-event, see his comment to Neal Oxenhandler, p. 268.

21. Gayle Ormiston and Alan Schrift, eds., *The Hermeneutic Tradition: From Ast to Ricoeur* and *Transforming the Hermeneutic Context: The French Connection* (Albany: State University of New York Press, 1990).

22. John D. Caputo, *Radical Hermeneutics* (Bloomington: Indiana University Press, 1987).

23. "Gadamer and Derrida as Interpreters of Heidegger: Four Texts of Gadamer and Four Texts of Derrida," in *The Question of Hermeneutics* ed. Timothy J. Stapleton (The Hague: Kluwer Academic Publishers, 1994), pp. 255–305, especially p. 305.

24. See his essay in *Dieter Stöver: 1922–1984* (Oldenburg: Oldenburg Landesmuseum, 1990).

25. For the bibliography in *The Philosophy of Hans-Georg Gadamer* cited above, I assembled for the first time a list of Gadamer's radio and television broadcasts in Germany from 1949 to the present. See pp. 588–99 in that volume. These interviews are preserved on archival tapes and inexpensively available to scholars.

26. See the second appendix for full publication data on all the books in English mentioned in this paragraph.

27. It is not the sole representative of that genre available in English. Several important interviews form an integral part of *Hans-Georg Gadamer on Education, Poetry, and History: Applied Hermeneutics* (1992), edited by Dieter Misgeld and Graeme Nicholson, and many interviews have been published in scholarly journals. See Makita's *Gadamer-Bibliographie*, pp. 219–44.

28. This is the deeper meaning of experience, as Gadamer argues in a significant section of *TM*, 346–62: "The Concept of Experience (*Erfahrung*) and the Essence of the Hermeneutic Experience."

29. *Aus der Erfahrung des Denkens* (Pfullingen: Neske, 1954), 27 pp. According to Gadamer, these were written when Heidegger was receiving treatment for depression and they cannot be taken seriously as poetry. To me, they seem to be Heidegger taking the logical next step and expressing himself in poetry.

30. See vols. 8 and 9 of his *Gesammelte Werke*, titled *Aesthetik und Poetik* I and II, and especially volume 9, subtitled *Hermeneutik im Vollzug* [*Hermeneutics in*

Performance] (Tübingen: Mohr Siebeck, 1993). The ten-volume set is now available in an inexpensive paperbound edition.

31. See Schleiermacher, *Hermeneutics: The Handwritten Manuscripts*, ed. Heinz Kimmerle and trans. James Duke and Jack Forstman (Missoula, Montana: Scholars Press, 1977); and Schleiermacher, "Aphorisms on Hermeneutics from 1805 and 1809/10" and "Hermeneutics: Outline of the 1819 Lectures," in *The Hermeneutic Tradition*, edited by Gayle L. Ormiston and Alan D. Schrift (Albany: State University of New York Press, 1990), pp. 57–84 and 85–100. See also Schleiermacher, *Dialectic, or the Art of Doing Philosophy* (Albany: Scholars Press, 1996), and Martin Redeker, *Schleiermacher: His Life and Thought* (Philadelphia: Fortress Press, 1977). Recently, *Hermeutik und Kritik* (1838) has been translated in Friedrich Schleiermacher, *Hermeneutics and Criticism and Other Writings*, ed. and trans. Andrew Bowie (Cambridge: Cambridge University Press, 1998).

32. *Dialogue and Deconstruction*, p. 110.

33. His is another face of Socrates. See James Risser, "The Two Faces of Socrates: Gadamer/Derrida," in *Dialogue and Deconstruction*, pp. 176–185.

34. Regarding Derrida's search for infrastructures, see Rodophe Gasché, *The Tain of the Mirror: Deconstruction and the Philosophy of Reflection* (Cambridge: Harvard University Press, 1986).

35. Translated in *Dialogue and Deconstruction*, pp. 52–57.

36. "Good Will to Understand and the Will to Power," in *Dialogue and Deconstruction*, pp. 162–75.

37. Translated in *Dialogue and Deconstruction*, pp. 58–71.

38. See Neal Oxenhandler's essay, "The Man with Shoes of Wind: The Derrida–Gadamer Encounter," in *Dialogue and Deconstruction*, pp. 265–68.

39. See "Reply to Jacques Derrida," *Dialogue and Deconstruction*, pp. 55–57.

40. *Hermeneutik-Ästhetik-Praktische Philosophie: Hans-Georg Gadamer im Gespräch*, ed. Carsten Dutt (Heidelberg: Carl Winter, 1st ed. 1993, 2nd ed. 1995, 3rd ed. 2000). A promising book by Dutt is *Gadamer und die Dichter: Poetologische, interpretationstheoretische und interpretationspraktische Konsequenzen einer philosophischen Hermeneutik* (2001).

41. *Wahrheit und Methode: Grundzürge einer philosophischen Hermeneutik* (Tübingen: J. C. B. Mohr 1960). Volume one of his ten-volume *Gesammelte Werke* (Tübingen: Mohr Siebeck, 1986).

42. The supplements appear in the English translations. For full publication data on all book-length publications in English by and about Gadamer, see the bibliographical appendices.

43. On this topic see also Gadamer's lengthy article, "Die Phänomenologische Bewegung," which he first published in the *Philosophische Rundschau* 11

(1964): 1–45, a journal Gadamer edited with Helmut Kuhn for two decades beginning in 1950. A translation, "The Phenomenological Movement," appeared in Hans-Georg Gadamer, *Philosophical Hermeneutics*, translated and edited by David E. Linge (Berkeley: University of California Press, 1976), pp. 130–181.

44. Dermot Moran, "Hans-Georg Gadamer: Philosophical Hermeneutics," in *Introduction to Phenomenology* (London: Routledge, 2000), pp. 248–86.

45. Munich: Kösel, 1987. Paperback: DTV, 1991.

46. Hamburg: Argument Verlag, 1995.

47. See especially pp. 11–15 of the "Reflections" in *The Philosophy of Hans-Georg Gadamer*, for his detailed account of his few writings during the Hitler period and references to the desperate circumstances of the time during the Hitler period and immediately after the war, as well as Grondin, chs. 7–11, pp. 131–260.

48. A book-length study of his philosophical thought during this period is Robert R. Sullivan's *Political Hermeneutics: The Early Thinking of Hans-Georg Gadamer* (University Park: Pennsylvania State University Press, 1989). It, too, does not in any way identify Gadamer's thought with Nazi ideology, an absurd idea.

49. "Reflections," p. 14.

50. Ibid., p. 13.

51. Tübingen: Mohr Siebeck, 1999.

52. See Richard Wolin, "Nazism and the Complicities of Hans-Georg Gadamer: Untruth and Method," *The New Republic*, May 15, 2000, pp. 36–45.

53. *Gadamer-Bibliographie (1922–1994)*. Makita is continually updating his 1995 bibliography. See www.ms.kuki.sut.ac.jp/KMSLab/makita/neuers.html.

Preface to Part I

1. Translator note: Dutt's notes have been retained. Where further information in the text or in the notes has been added by the translator, this has been either bracketed or, in the case of added informational footnotes, indicated by the notation "Translator note." Obvious translator additions are sometimes indicated with parentheses for smoothness. Parenthetical citations of Gadamer's writings in the text will refer to the collected works in ten volumes published between 1985 and 1995 by J. C. B. Mohr (Paul Siebeck). They will use the abbreviation *GW* [*Gesammelte Werke*]. The full publication data for Gadamer's masterwork, *Truth and Method* is as follows: Hans-Georg Gadamer, *Gesammelte Werke*, vol. 1: *Hermeneutik I: Wahrheit und Methode: Grundzüge einer philosophischen Hermeneutik* (Tübingen: J. C. B. Mohr [Paul Siebeck], 1986). The subtitle *Elements of a Philosophical Hermeneutics* is omitted in the English translations. Where an English translation of a citation is available, the translator has

added it and the page number. The wording may differ, however, since all quotations have been translated directly from the German along with the rest of the text. The full publication data for Gadamer's *Truth and Method* is: *Truth and Method*, translated by Garrett Barden and John Cumming in the 1st edition [1975]; for 2nd revised edition in 1989 the translation was reviewed and revised by Joel Weinsheimer and Donald G. Marshall (New York: Crossroad, 1989).

2. See "Selbstdarstellung" in the *Gesammelte Werke* 2 (1986): 479–508, here citing from p. 498. [For the English translation see "Reflections on My Philosophical Journey," the autobiographical sketch in *The Philosophy of Hans-Georg Gadamer*, ed. Lewis H. Hahn (LaSalle, Ill.: Open Court Press, 1997), pp. 3–18, 26–40, with this specific citation coming from p. 30.]

Chapter 1: Hermeneutics

1. *De doctrina christiana* in *Patrologia latina*, ed. Jacques-Paul Migne, XXXIV, Paris 1845, Book III, ch. 1,1, p. 65. [Rough translation: Man, fear God, will to diligently inquire into the Holy Scriptures.] [All notes in the first three conversations are those of Carsten Dutt unless square-bracketed, marked as "translator's note," or merely a translator reference to an English translation.]

2. Along with *Being and Time* see the early Heidegger lecture-course, *Ontologie—Hermeneutik der Faktizität*, ed. Käte Bröcker-Oltmanns, *Gesamtausgabe* 63 (Frankfurt: Klostermann, 1988)/Martin Heidegger, *Ontology—The Hermeneutics of Facticity*, trans. John van Buren (Bloomington: Indiana University Press, 1999).

3. Georg Misch, *Lebensphilosophie und Phänomenologie. Eine Auseinandersetzung der Diltheyschen Richtung mit Heidegger und Husserl*. Bonn, 1930. [Leipzig: Teubner, 1931 and Darmstadt: Wissenschaftliche Buchgesellschaft, 1975.] [This assertion is not to deny Dilthey's own interest in hermeneutics but rather to deal with its influence on the later Dilthey school.]

4. Translator's note: This German term, literally "sciences of the [human] spirit," defies translation. We will sometimes render it "human sciences," sometimes leave it in the German as a technical term. It includes both the humanities and the social sciences, all those disciplines that deal with human activities and the "imprints" of human activities, e.g., the fine arts, literature, history, religion, philosophy, and even social sciences, politics, and economics.

5. See his *Erläuterungen zu Hölderlins Dichtung* (Frankfurt: Klostermann, 1952), pp. 36 ff. /*Elucidations of Hölderlin's Poetry*, translated by Keith Hoeller (Amherst, N.Y.: Humanity Press, 2000), pp. 54–55.

6. See Ernst Tugendhat's review, "The Fusion of Horizons," in the *Times Literary Supplement* 19 May 1978, p. 165; reprinted in Ernst Tugendhat, *Philosophische Aufsätze* (Frankfurt: Suhrkamp, 1992), pp. 426–32, this citation p. 428.

7. This term and concept can be traced back to Max Scheler and the distinctions he develops in *Die Wissensformen und die Gesellschaft* (1926). See the 2nd ed. with supplements, edited by Maria Scheler (Bern & Munich, 1960) [same as his *Gesammelte Werke* 8], pp. 200–11.

8. Translator's note: This is also quite true in English. How does one have a dialogue with "tradition"? Just for this reason, I have generally translated *Tradition* in German with "tradition" and *Überlieferung* as "that which has been handed down to us," or "our heritage," depending on what sounds most natural in the context.

9. See *GW* 1:302/*TM* 296–297: "Understanding is in truth not an understanding better, neither in the sense of understanding something better in a subject-matter through clearer ideas, nor in the sense of the basic superiority that the conscious mind has over what is unconsciously produced. It suffices to say that one understands *differently if one understands at all.*"

10. Translator's note: This difficult sentence in German reads: "Die Tradition ist die Vermittlung ihrer und des von ihr Vermittelten doch nur in ihr und für sie selbst." Manfred Frank, *Das individuelle Allgemeine* (Frankfurt: Suhrkamp, 1985), pp. 20–34, citation is on p. 33.

11. Ibid.

12. "Vom Wesen der Erfahrung" ["On the Nature of Experience"], in *Anthropologische Forschung*, 1961, pp. 26–43; citations are from pp. 41 and 37.

13. *GW* 1: 361/*TM* 355, bottom line. "The dialectic of experience culminates not in a knowing that closes the books, so to speak, but in bringing about a space of openness for experience, a bringing that is brought about by experience itself."

14. "Die Aufgabe der Geisteswissenschaften in der modernen Gesellschaft" in Joachim Ritter, *Subjektivität* (Frankfurt: Suhrkamp, 1980), pp. 105–40. Citations in this paragraph are from pp. 132–33.

15. See Odo Marquard, "Über die Unvermeidlichkeit der Geisteswissenschaften," in his *Apologie des Zufälligen* (Stuttgart: 1986), pp. 98–116, this citation was from p. 105.

16. In Plato's *Republic, dianoia* is the path of reasoning leading up to the forms of the Beautiful and Good. Translator note.

17. Translator's note: The German is "alle Formen menschlicher Lebensgemeinschaft."

18. "Alle Lebensgemeinschaften sind Sprachgemeinschaften, und Sprache ist nur im Gespräch." Translator's note: This deep and luminous sentence resists translation, so I have gone beyond a literal rendering, which would be: "All life-communities are speech-communities, and language is only language in conversation."

19. "Vereinsamung als Symptom von Selbstentfremdung," in *Lob der Theorie* (Frankfurt: Suhrkamp, 1983), pp. 123–38. / "Loneliness as a Symptom of Self-Alienation," in *Praise of Theory*, trans. Chris Dawson (Yale University Press, 1998), pp. 115–30.

20. *Wer bin Ich und wer bist Du?* (Frankfurt: Suhrkamp, 1973), pp. 10–13 and especially pp. 34–44. This short book along with Gadamer's other essays on Celan appears in *Gadamer on Celan: "Who am I and who are you?" and Other Essays* (Albany: State University of New York Press, 1997). *Gadamer on Celan* was also briefly available on the Internet, but only to subscribers as an eBook at www.netlibrary.com.

21. *Nietzsche* (Pfullingen: Neske, 1961), 1: 578–579/Heidegger, *Nietzsche*, translated by Joan Stambaugh, David Farrell Krell, and Frank Capuzzi, vol. 3: *The Will to Power as Knowledge* (San Francisco: Harper, 1987), pp. 90–91.

22. "Aus einem Gespräch von der Sprache," in Martin Heidegger, *Unterwegs zur Sprache* (Pfullingen: Neske, 1959), pp. 83–155, here pp. 151–152/"A Dialogue on Language," in Martin Heidegger, *On the Way to Language*, trans. Peter D. Hertz (New York: Harper & Row, 1971), pp. 1–54, here pp. 51–52.

23. "Die Aufgabe der Philosophy," in *Das Erbe Europas* (Frankfurt: Suhrkamp, 1989), pp. 166–173, here pp. 172–73.

Chapter 2: Aesthetics

1. Translator's note: This was at a conference on the topic of "Text and Interpretation" at the Goethe Institute, Paris, April 25–27, 1981, called by Philippe Forget, where Gadamer and Derrida and four other major scholars presented papers. Derrida made a brief reply overnight to Gadamer's paper, to which Gadamer also responded briefly. This brief exchange was the "encounter," in the strict sense, but the longer paper presented by each is also a part of the encounter. Gadamer's paper, along with Derrida's reply and Gadamer's answer but not Derrida's paper, was first published in French as "Le défi herméneutique" in the *Réview internationale de philosophie* 38, nr. 151 (1984): 325–40. For its publication in German, Gadamer added the last third of its present text and retitled it "Text und Interpretation."

2. *Text und Interpretation: Eine deutsche-französische Debatte mit Beiträgen von Jacques Derrida, Philippe Forget, Manfred Frank, Hans-Georg Gadamer, Jean Greisch und François Laruelle*, ed. Philippe Forget (Munich: Wilhelm Fink, 1984).

3. *Dialogue and Deconstruction: The Gadamer-Derrida Encounter*, translated & edited by Diane P. Michelfelder and Richard E. Palmer (Albany: State University of New York Press, 1989). (Translator's note: Hereinafter cited as *Dialogue and Deconstruction* or *DD*. In addition to the essays by Jacques Derrida and Hans-Georg Gadamer, and their brief replies to each other's contributions, this

volume contains four additional later essays by Professor Gadamer on deconstruction, and commentary essays by Fred Dallmayr, Philippe Forget, Manfred Frank, Josef Simon, James Risser, Charles Shepherdson, G. B. Madison, Herman Rapaport, Donald G. Marshall, Richard Shusterman, David Farrell Krell, Robert Bernasconi, John Sallis, John D. Caputo, Neal Oxenhandler, and Gabe Eisenstein. A fifth essay on deconstruction, "Hermeneutik auf der Spur" [1994], was published by Gadamer later, and appears in *GW* 10 [1995]: 148–74.)

4. "Text und Interpretation," in *GW* 2 (1986): 333/*DD*, p. 24. Second quote can be found in *GW* 2 (1986): 372/*DD*, p. 113.

5. Translator's note: However, the complete audiotapes of the conference are archived by West Deutsche Rundfunk. These may be obtained for scholarly use from Ulrich Boehm, WDR. See my bibliographical entry under: 1988, 3— RD—"Martin Heidegger: die philosophische und politische Dimension seines Denkens," in *The Philosophy of Hans-Georg Gadamer*, ed. Lewis E. Hahn (La-Salle, Ill.: Open Court, 1997), p. 596, for further information, including the WDR address. Participants were: Jacques Derrida, Philippe Lacoue-Labarthe, Gadamer, and Reiner Wiehl. I believe Gadamer's article, "Über die Politische Inkompetenz der Philosophie," in *Sinn und Form: Beiträge zur Literatur*, 45.1 (1993): 37–52, deals with this issue. Also, there was an article on the conference in the *Frankfurter Allgemeine Zeitung*.

6. Translator's note: The late Hans-Robert Jauss was a well-known literary historian at the University Konstanz, Germany, and a member of the "Hermeneutik und Poetik Arbeitsgruppe" which took up the banner of hermeneutics in the early 1960s and published biennial volumes for over three decades. Important among his early programmatic writings was "Literaturgeschichte als Provokation der Literaturwissenschaft," in *Literaturgeschichte als Provocation* (Frankfurt: Suhrkamp, 1970), which was tranlated into English by Elizabeth Benzinger as "Literary History as a Challenge to Literary Theory," *New Literary History* 2,1 (Autumn 1970): 7–37. See also his *Toward an Aesthetic of Reception*, trans. Timothy Bahti (Minneapolis: University of Minnesota Press, 1985). Other members of the Konstanz group taking up the banner of reception-aesthetics were Wolfgang Iser and Rainer Warning. See Iser's books, *The Implied Reader* (Baltimore: The Johns Hopkins University Press, 1974) and *The Act of Reading: A Theory of Aesthetic Response* (Baltimore: The Johns Hopkins Press, 1978).

7. Translator's note: Herman Grimm lived from 1828 to 1901 and published prolifically in the area of art history. His book *Das Leben Raphaels* was a translation of the Italian text by Vasari (Berlin: Dümmlers Verlag, 1872). It was followed by an expanded 515-page second edition in 1886, a third edition in 1896, and subsequent editions. A complete edition was edited by Ludwig Goldschneider (Vienna: Phaidon Verlag, 1931). It was already translated into En-

glish from the German in 1888 by Sarah Holland Adams as *The Life of Raphael* (Boston: Cupples & Hurd, 1888).

8. As we see in Rainer Warning, "Zur Hermeneutik des Klassischen," in *Über das Klassische*, ed. Rudolf Bockholdt (Frankfurt: Suhrkamp, 1987), 77–100, citation here from p. 86.

9. "Hans-Robert Jauss, "Literaturgeschichte als Provokation der Literatur-wissenschaft," pp. 187ff.

10. Ibid., p. 188.

11. See *GW* 1 (1986): 292. "The classical does not designate a quality of corresponding to a determinate historical phenomenon, but rather the extraordinary way of itself being historical (*Geschichtlichsein*), the historical advantage of preservation, which in ever-renewed acts of preservation, lets a truth [*ein Wahres*, related to *Bewahren*) be." Dutt note: On Gadamer's concept of 'letting-being', see the following explanation in *The Relevance of the Beautiful:* "What it comes down to is *allowing what is to be* [*das, was ist, sein zu lassen*]. But to 'let-be' [*Seinlassen*] does not mean only repeating what one already knows. One lets what was be, not in the form of a lived experience of repetition [*Wiederholungserlebnis*], but through letting oneself be determined by the encounter itself." *Die Aktualität des Schönen* (Stuttgart: Reclam, 1977), p. 65; *The Relevance of the Beautiful and Other Essays*, translated by Nicholas Walker, edited by Robert Bernasconi (New York: Cambridge University Press, 1986), p. 49. Hereafter cited as *AS* and *RB*.

12. Hans-Robert Jauss, *Ästhetische Erfahrung und literarische Hermeneutik* (Frankfurt: 1982), p. 791. [The original German of this difficult sentence reads: "Klassisch ist, was sich bewahrt, weil es sich selber bedeutet und sich selber deutet ... das der jeweiligen Gegenwart etwas so sagt, als sei es eigens ihr gesagt."] English: *Aesthetic Experience and Literary Hermeneutics*, trans. Michael Shaw (Minneapolis: University of Minnesota Press, 1982).

13. Translator's note: Dutt's reference here is to Jauss's well-known efforts to describe the *Urpublikum* (original public) of works written in the Middle Ages, and to reconstruct the effect of the work on this public. While this may be a valid project, it is misleading to see this as an application of Gadamer's hermeneutics, since Gadamer's interest is in the effect on the present interpreter.

14. See Rodolphe Gasché, *The Tain of the Mirror: Derrida and the Philosophy of Reflection* (Cambridge: Harvard University Press, 1986).

15. "Sprache und Verstehen" (1970), *GW* 2: 184–98 (not yet translated into English).

16. Jacques Derrida, *Grammatologie*, trans. Hans-Jörg Rheinberger and Hanns Zischler (Frankfurt: Suhrkamp, 1988), p. 35; *Of Grammatology*, trans. Gayatri Chakravorty Spivak (Baltimore: The Johns Hopkins University Press, 1974), p. 15.

17. See Richard Rorty, "From Ironist Theory to Private Allusions: Derrida," in his *Contingency, Irony, and Solidarity* (New York: Cambridge University Press, 1989), pp. 122–37. Citation on p. 125.

18. *La Voix et le phénomène* (Paris: PUF, 1967). (Translation: *Speech and Phenomena and Other Essays on Husserl's Theory of Signs* (Evanston: Northwestern University Press, 1973).

19. "Three Questions to Hans-Georg Gadamer," translated by Diane Michelfelder and Richard Palmer in *DD* 52–54, this ref. p. 53. Translator's note: French original title is: "Bonnes Volontés de Puissance (Une Réponse à Hans-Georg Gadamer)," ("Good Will to Power [A Response to Hans-Georg Gadamer]") and was published in *Révue internationale de philosophie* 38, nr. 151 (1984): 344 f. along with only the first part of Gadamer's essay, "Le défi herméneutique," translated by Philippe Forget, pp. 340, and without Derrida's essay, which only appeared much later in a six-hundred-fifty-page collection of his writings titled *Psyché: inventions de l'autre* (Paris: Galilée, 1987).

20. *Nicht gegen die Sprache, sondern mit der Sprache denken*. Translator's note: See Gadamer's late essay, "Mit der Sprache Denken" (1990), *GW* 10:346–353. Translated as the "Travelling Scholar" section of "Reflections on My Philosophical Journey," in *The Philosophy of Hans-Georg Gadamer*, pp. 18–25.

21. "Text und Interpretation," in *GW* 2:330–360, citation 351–352/*DD* 21–51, citation 41–42. See also "The Eminent Text and Its Truth," originally published in English translation by Geoffrey Waite in *The Bulletin of the Midwest Modern Language Association* 13.1 (1980): 3–10, discussion 11–23. The German text is a reworked and enlarged version and appears in the collected works without the discussion. See "Der eminente Text und seine Wahrheit," *GW* 8 (1993): 286–295. Translator note.

22. "Ende der Kunst?" in *Das Erbe Europas* (Frankfurt: Suhrkamp, 1989), p. 82. Translator's note: In *GW* 8:206–220. Untranslated. On the topic of reading, see also *TM* 160–161, 191, 268–269, 340, 391–92.

23. This is a book in which Gadamer wrote an introduction when it was published as an inexpensive paperback: "Zur Einführung" in Martin Heidegger, *Der Ursprung des Kunstwerkes* (Stuttgart: Reclam, 1960), pp. 93–114; translated as "Heidegger's Later Philosophy," in *Philosophical Hermeneutics*, ed. David E. Linge (Berkeley: University of California Press, 1976), 213–28. "The Origin of the Work of Art" may be found in Martin Heidegger, *Poetry, Language, and Thought*, trans. and intro. by Albert Hofstadter (Harper & Row, 1971), pp. 17–87.

24. *Die Aktualität des Schönen* (*AS* 45/*RB* 34). Also, *GW* 8: 125.

25. Ibid.

26. Martin Heidegger, *Der Ursprung des Kunstwerkes*.

27. "I don't know what." [A well-known phrase in the aesthetics of the French enlightenment, pointing to the inexplicability of the beautiful.]

28. In English we say: Do you *read* me? Translator note.

29. *Wieder-auf-den-Text-Zurückkommen.*

30. *Vollzugswahrheit* = a truth that emerges only in the carrying out of interpretation. The two essays to which he refers are "Wort und Bild—'so wahr, so seiend'" (*GW* 8:373–99), and "Zur Phänomenologie von Ritual und Sprache" (*GW* 400–40). I have discussed these two works in my essay "Ritual, Rightness, and Truth in Two Late Works of Hans-Georg Gadamer," in *The Philosophy of Hans-Georg Gadamer*, pp. 529–47. I have also translated but not published the first of these essays and written a summarizing and interpretive essay on the second in "Gadamer's Recent Work on Language and Philosophy: On 'Zur Phänomenologie von Ritual und Sprache'" in the recent Gadamer issue of *Continental Philosophy Review* 33 (2000): 381–93. Vol. 9 of the *GW*, dedicated to the concrete interpreting of individual authors and works, carries the title *Hermeneutik im Vollzug—Hermeneutics Carried Out*, or *Hermeneutics in Performance*. Translator's note.

31. [In German: "eine absterbenden ästhetischen Kultur."] See "Sein Geist Gott" in *GW* 3: 320–32; citation here is from p. 330/"Being Spirit God" in Hans-Georg Gadamer, *Heidegger's Ways*, translated by John W. Stanley and introduced by Dennis J. Schmidt (Albany: State University of New York Press, 1994), pp. 181–95, citation here ca. p. 192.

Chapter 3: Practical Philosophy

1. "Über die politische Inkompetenz der Philosophie," *Sinn und Form* 45 (1993): 5–12, citation comes from p. 11. [Based on a speech Gadamer originally gave in Italy in 1988. The Beaufret reference can be found near the beginning of Heidegger's "Letter on Humanism," where he refers to Beaufret's letter, which asks him: "When are you going to write an ethics?"]

2. Translator note: See also Dante, *Purgatorio* Canto XV, lines 61–75, where Virgil explains that in sharing spiritual things, unlike material things, partnership does not diminish each share but increases it.

3. See "Was ist Praxis? Die Bedingungen gesellschaftlicher Vernunft" in *Vernunft im Zeitalter der Wissenschaft* [*VZW*], pp. 54–77, citation here is from p. 60. Also in *GW* 4: 216–28, citation on p. 219/"What is Practice? The Conditions of Social Reason" in Gadamer's *Reason in the Age of Science*, translated by Frederick G. Lawrence (Cambridge: MIT Press, 1981), pp. 88–112, citation p. 74.

4. Translator's note: Horkheimer, Adorno, Marcuse, and Habermas are leading representatives of this school.

5. "Was ist Praxis?" Ibid., p. 67/"What is Practice," p. 80.

6. "Platos Denken in Utopien" (1983), in *GW* 7: 270–89. [Reference is to Sir Karl Popper's *The Open Society and its Enemies*. Vol. 1: *The Spell of Plato;* vol. 2: *Prophecy: Hegel, Marx, and the Aftermath* (London: Routledge, 1945, fifth edition 1966; also published by Princeton University Press).]

7. Translator's note: So it is not Athens that Plato has in mind in the *Republic* but Syracuse and Dionysus II. Professor Gadamer added this clarification in conversation with the translator, August 7, 1998.

8. "Was ist Praxis? Die Bedingungen gesellschaftlicher Vernunft," in *VZW,* p. 70. In *GW* 4: 216–28. See note 3 for English translation.

9. Translator's note: Professor Gadamer has in mind Bloch's three volume classic, *Das Prinzip der Hoffnung* (Frankfurt: Suhrkamp, 1959, 1969)/ *The Principle of Hope*, three volumes, translated by Neville and Stephen Paice and Paul Knight (Cambridge: MIT Press, 1995). He probably also read the earlier work by Bloch, *Geist der Utopie* (Berlin: P. Cassirer, 1923), recently translated as *The Spirit of Utopia*, trans. Anthony A. Nassar (Stanford, Calif.: Stanford University Press, 2000).

Chapter 4: The Greeks, Our Teachers

1. Translator's note: Glenn Most is a professor of classical philology at the University of Heidelberg. The German text was published as follows: Hans-Georg Gadamer, "'Die Griechen, unsere Lehrer.' Ein Gespräch mit Glenn W. Most." *Internationale Zeitschrift für Philosophie* 1 (1994): 139–49.

2. Translator's note: Paul Friedländer fled the Nazis and continued his scholarly work in New Zealand. A translation of his great three-volume Plato book soon appeared: *Plato: An Introduction* and *Plato: The Dialogues of the 2nd and 3rd Periods*, trans. Hans Meyerhoff in the Bollingen Series, 3 vols. (New York: Pantheon, 1958, 1969).

3. Translator's note: See Werner Jeager, *Paideia: The Ideals of Greek Culture*, trans. Gilbert Highet (New York: Oxford University Press, 1944). The German original, in three successive volumes, was published in Berlin by de Gruyter, in 1934, 1936, and 1944.

4. Translator's note: See Helmut Kuhn, "Humanismus in der Gegenwart: Zu Werner Jaegers Werk *Paideia: Die Formung des griechischen Menschen*," in *Kant-Studien* 29 (1934): 328-38.

Chapter 5: On Phenomenology

1. Translator's note: Alfons Grieder is a professor of sociology at the City University of London. His conversation with Gadamer took place at the University of Freiburg on September 30, 1992. The interview was tape-recorded in

German, translated by Grieder himself and reviewed by Professor Gadamer in Heidelberg before its publication in the *Journal of the British Society for Phenomenology* 26, 2 (May 1995): 116–26. The following twenty-two explanatory notes are by Grieder. I have made a half-dozen minor stylistic changes to smooth the flow or clarify the meaning.

2. Gadamer had taken up his studies at Marburg University in 1918.

3. Richard Hamann (1879–1961) was professor at Marburg University from 1913 to 1949. His philosophical outlook was partly based on Wilhelm Dilthey and Georg Simmel.

4. From Johann Wilhelm von Goethe, "Selige Sehnsucht," *Westösterlicher Divan*.

5. E. Husserl, "Ideen zu einer reinen Phänomenologie und phänomenologischen Philosophie," *Jahrbuch für Philosophy und phänomenologische Forschung*, vol. 1, Halle, 1913.

6. Paul Natorp (1854–1924) taught philosophy and pedagogies at Marburg University, where he was professor beginning in 1885.

7. *Dilthey-Jahrbuch fur Philosophie und Geschichte der Geisteswissenschaften* 6 (1989): 237–54.

8. See Hans-Georg Gadamer, "Heidegger's 'theologische' Jugendschrift," *Dilthey-Jahrbuch* 6: 228–34. [Translator's note: Much of Heidegger's posthumous work has been published since 1992, of course, so Gadamer today would soften the claim he makes here.]

9. Hans-Georg Gadamer, *Philosophische Lehrjahre: Eine Rückschau* (Frankfurt: Klostermann, 1977). *Philosophical Apprenticeships*, trans. Robert R. Sullivan (Cambridge: The MIT Press, 1985).

10. Aristotle, *Nicomachean Ethics*, Book VI, 11449. In English the phrase is frequently translated as "the eye of the soul," in German sometimes as "das Auge des Geistes" [the eye of the mind].

11. A play on words, with "ideas" referring to Husserl's book *Ideas* (*Ideen zu einer reinen Phänomenologie und phänomenologischen Philosophie* [1913]). [Translation of " Ideas I": *Ideas: General Introduction to Pure Phenomenology*, trans. W. R. Boyce Gibson (New York: Collier Books, 1962).

12. Paul Friedländer, classical philologist, professor at Marburg University. [Author of a masterful three-volume study, *Plato: An Introduction* and *Plato: The Dialogues of the 2nd and 3rd Periods*, trans. Hans Meyerhoff in the Bollingen Series (New York: Pantheon, 1958, 1969).]

13. Gadamer is referring to "Der aristotelische *Protreptikos* und die entwicklungsgeschichtliche Betrachtung der aristotelischen Ethik," first published in 1928, now in *GW* 5 (1985): 164–86. Werner Jaeger was a leading Aristotle scholar, especially known for his investigations into Aristotle's philosophical

development (see, e.g., his *Aristotle: Fundamentals of the History of his Develop-ment*). [Translator's note: He was popularly known also for his *Paideia: The Ideals of Greek Culture: Archaic Greece and the Mind of Athens*, trans. Gilbert Highet (New York: Oxford University Press, 1963).]

14. In Gadamer's view, the violation of the Munich Agreement had a deci-sive influence on the subsequent course of, and relation between, British and German philosophy.

15. [Translator's note: This was a topic Jeff Malpas was exploring in Heidel-berg in 1996, especially the parallels between Davidson and Gadamer.]

16. E. Husserl, *Vorlesungen zur Phänomenologie des inneren Zeitbewusstseins*, ed. Martin Heidegger, in *Jahrbuch für Philosophie und phänomenologische For-schung*, vol. 8 (Halle, 1928). [The most recent English translation is *On the Phe-nomenology of the Consciousness of Internal Time*, trans. John Barnett Brough (Dordrecht: Kluwer Academic Publishers, 1992)].

17. From 1939 to 1947 Gadamer was professor at the University of Leipzig. The physicist Werner Heisenberg also taught there from 1927 to 1941.

18. See especially "Antike Atomtheorie," first published in 1935, now in *GW* 5 (1985): 263–79.

19. Georg Misch, *Lebensphilosophie und Phänomenologie* (Leipzig, Tuebner, 1931). The following year a second edition was published. Translator's note: Reissued by Darmstadt: Wissenschaftliche Buchgesellschaft, 1975.

20. See M. Heidegger, *Hölderlins Hymnen "Germanien" und "Der Rhein"* (Frankfurt: Klostermann, 1980 [2nd revised edition 1989, *Gesamtausgabe*, vol. 39]).

21. *Truth and Method* [*GW* 1], pp. 167–68, 235–40, 258–61.

22. Gonsoeth was also well aware of the second element, the historical *hori-zon* of (scientific) understanding.

23. Max Scheler (1874–1928), although Husserl was critical of his work, ex-erted a considerable influence, e.g., on Heidegger (who dedicated his Kant book to Scheler) and on Nicolai Hartmann, especially his *Ethics*. Adolf Reinach (1883–1917) was part of the Göttingen Circle, where he was held in high es-teem, not least by Husserl himself. Theodor Lipps (1851–1914) taught at Mu-nich, where Reinach was among his students.

Chapter 6: "The real nazis . . . "

1. This conversation was originally published as "' . . . die wirklichen Nazis hatten doch überhaupt kein Interesse an uns' : Hans-Georg Gadamer im Ge-spräch mit Dörte von Westernhagen" in *Das Argument: Zeitschrift für Philoso-phie und Sozialwissenschaften* [Hamburg], issue no. 182, vol. 32, 4 (July-Aug. 1990): 543–55. The editorial note served there as an introduction to the text of

the interview. The parenthetical documentation notes in the text refer to works that Westernhagen lists in a bibliography at the end of the interview. The years of publication given by her have been retained in the parenthetical references. The translator has supplied all information provided by the bibliography, and occasionally where page numbers of articles were not given, these have been silently supplied by the translator. Organization names used in the interview have generally been translated into English, but not the names of German periodicals. Some modifications of the endnotes that do not affect their meaning have been made, such as adding words like "was" to verbless sentences and placing the source of quotes before the citation instead of in the parentheses, with the page number supplied in the parentheses after the quote. Informational endnotes added by the translator have been appropriately indicated, and additional data when supplied in notes is indicated with brackets. Otherwise, all notes and publication data have been supplied by Dörte von Westernhagen.

2. Translator's note: J. Grondin gives the dates as 1934–35 in *Hans-Georg Gadamer: Eine Biographie* (Tübingen: Mohr, 1999), p. 378.

3. Richard Kroner (1884–1974), a full professor at Kiel from 1929 to 1934, was until 1933 editor of the journal *Logos*. As a "frontline fighter" he fell first under the exceptions clause of the "Law for the Reconstruction of the Civil Service" (7.4.1933). But when Nazi students broke up his lecture on 15 January 1934, he was compulsorily transferred to Frankfurt and at the end of 1935 was released in accordance with the Nürenberg Laws ("Reich Citizens Law"). He emigrated to the USA via Great Britain in 1939. (See Asmus 1990.)

4. Kurt Hildebrandt (1881–1966), 1932 Director of the Berlin-Herzberge Sanitarium, 1933 NSDAP (National-Socialist German Workers Party), took over the teaching position of Julius Stenzel (1883–1935), who after student pressure was compulsorily transfered to Halle. From 1935–1938 he was editor of the *Zeitschrift für die gesamte Naturwissenschaft*. (See Goldschmidt 1985.)

5. [Frankfurt: Klostermann, 1977.]

6. [*Norm und Entartung des Menschen* (Dresden: Sibyllen-Verlag, 1920). There were subsequent editions also.]

7. Ernst Cassirer (1874–1945) emigrated in May 1933 via Austria to Great Britain and in 1941 to the USA. The chair was not filled. Cassirer's habilitated assistant Hermann Noack (1874–1977), who wanted to accompany his teacher into exile, functioned in his place at his request (see T. Cassirer 1981) and "during the time of National Socialism's rule took over the most important role in the Philosophical Seminar" (Meran 1990). Noack was Nov. 1933 a candidate for the SA, joined the NS Party in 1937, underwent "worldview" schooling in the regional school at Rissen. Under the "Political Union of the Faculties" and the People's University, he was taken from the Eastern Front and assigned

to the "Task Force Staff of Reich-leader Rosenberg" ["Einsatzstab Reichs-führer Rosenberg"]. He received his scheduled "extraordinary professorship" [*Extraordinat*], only in 1939 "after an unnerving tug-of-war among various of-fers." (Meran, ibid.)

8. Hans Heyse (1881–1976) became a member of the Party in 1933 and Rector of the University of Königsberg. He was professor in Göttingen from 1936–1945, and in 1937 leader of the Academy of Sciences there of the NS-Union of Teachers. Between 1935–1937 he chaired the Kant-Gesellschaft and served as editor of *Kant-Studien*. (See Dahms 1987)

9. Translator's note: He is well known as the author of the *Das Heilige* (*The Holy*) 1923, and other books.

10. Arnold Gehlen (1904–1976) became a member of the National Socialist Party as a private instructor in Leipzig. He became the substitute for the "cleansed" chair of Paul Tillich (Frankfurt 1933) and Hans Driesch (Leipzig 1934; from November on full professor). As occupant of the Kant chair of the Königsberg "University of the East" from 1938–1940, he was, according to the SS, "effective as a factor in the political activization of philosophy" (*Lagebericht des Sicherheitsdienstes der SS*, cited in Boberach 1965). After the annexation of the Eastern Reich, he became professor at the University of Vienna from 1940–1945. He also served as chair of the German Philosophical Society. (See Rüge-mer 1979, Klinger 1989)

11. Erich Rothacker (1888–1965), Professor of Philosophy, Sociology, and Psychology in Bonn.

12. Hans Freyer (1887–1969), professor in Leipzig from 1925 to 1948. He was in elected as "Leader" [*Führer*] of the German Society for Sociology. From 1938–1940 he was guest professor of German Cultural History in Budapest. There he had responsibility for directing the Foreign Office of the "German Scientific Institute" and according to Schelsky was "the most important advisor for the German military representatives in Budapest." (Schelsky 1981, 151) (See Muller 1987)

13. Oskar Becker (1889–1964), was professor in Bonn beginning in 1931. He was co-editor of Husserl's *Jahrbuch für Philosophie und Phänomenologische Forschung*. In Löwith's autobiography, written in 1940, he represented "Dr. B." as holding a racial doctrine that was at the outset "unpolitical," but nevertheless he maintained that it was "unconditionally necessary" that Germany dismiss the Jews "in order to eliminate the tremendous Jewish influence on German culture." (1986, 45–49)

14. Ludwig Ferdinand Clauss (1892–1974) was a coworker with Husserl in Freiburg from 1917–1921 and developed Husserl's intuition of essence [*Wesensschau*] into an ethnology of the souls of races [*Rassenseelenkunde*]. On account

of his Jewish wife, who was at the same time his coworker, from whom he separated in 1940, he could not join the National Socialist Party and had no academic career until 1945 (after which he became a professor in Frankfurt). At a working conference on Rosenberg's "Higher School" in 1941, Clauss—"who was entrusted by the Foreign Office with the high mission and had been sent abroad—was condemned by the leader of the Racial Politics Office of the NS-Party because he saw race as rooted in "soul and spirit" [*Seele und Geist*] instead of in the heritage, as his rival H. F. K. Günther held. "He had originally presented this doctrine as national-socialistic. He had in 1933–1934 successfully spoken at many Party meetings.

His lectures were especially popular among circles of students, of the BDM (*Bund deutscher Mädchen*), the Work Service organizations [1935–1945], thus among people who were seeking a genuine conviction and deepening, for whom the schematic Günther dogmatism did not appear to be appropriate to the times." (Cited by Poliakov/Wulf 1959, 414; on Clauss, Günther and the "two poles of racism in National Socialism," see Haug 1986, 58–66.)

15. Erich Frank (1883–1949) was the 1928 successor to Heidegger in Marburg. He was let go in 1935 on account of his Jewish descent. Emigrated to the United States in 1939.

16. Gottfried Feder (1883–1941) founded in 1918 the "German Union Struggling to Throw off the Bondage of Interest" and made this topic a main point in the original program of the NS-Party. "As spokesman for the earlier wing of the Party that was near to the people, and especially racist and anti-intellectual" (Wistrich 1987, 88), Feder's influence was radically curtailed in 1933 and he was finally shoved off into an honorary professorship in the Technische Hochschule in Berlin.

17. The "Declaration of College and University Professors for Adolf Hitler and the National-Socialist State" (Dresden, no publication year given) contains the speeches of a National-Socialist Union of Teachers meeting that took place on November 10, 1933, and about 1,000 signatures. As a "Call to the Cultured People of the World," it was sent out to foreign universities. The occasion for this was the plebiscite to support Hitler's withdrawal from the League of Nations and a single ticket of candidates for the Reichstag election. (See Poliakov/Wulf 1959, 104–108; on the role of Heidegger, see Farías 1989, 219–225).

18. Gerhard Krüger (1902–1972) was a private instructor in Marburg beginning in 1929 and in 1938 became professor. In 1940 he was compulsorily transferred to the University of Münster. Lisa Abendroth recalls, "At that time we students petitioned to the Professors Union to please leave Gerhard Krüger in Marburg, one wanted no others" (cited in Schneider 1977, 244). A professor of Romance Languages, Werner Krauss (1900–1976), became a private in-

structor in 1931 and became a professor at Marburg in 1942, but he was arrested by the Gestapo in the fall of 1942 on account of his membership in the Schulze-Boysen/Harnak Organization. A death sentence was lifted in 1944 after a clemency action on his behalf by the members and former members of the University. According to Schneider, "Former colleagues at Marburg like Hans-Georg Gadamer, who had gone to Leipzig in the middle thirties, his former teacher, Karl Vossler from Munich, and others, sent recommendations to the War Court of the Reich, and took other measures" (1977, 248).

19. According to the "Reichs-Habilitation Ordinance" of December 13, 1934, permission by the state to teach was made dependent on serving probation in a "Community Camp" [*Gemeinschaftslager*] arranged by the ministry of sciences. Gadamer writes, "I registered voluntarily for one such camp for my 'rehabilitation' and in the fall of 1936 went for several weeks to Weichselmünde in Danzig. I was lucky. The leader of the camp was a North German Count, a criminologist who felt himself a member of Greater Germany and who surely did not view Nazi Germany without some pains to his legal conscience. He looked at things completely from the point of view of foreign policy, from the national side. . . . Nevertheless, because of this 'rehabilitation' I gained an influential friend in this Count Gleispach, who in Berlin intervened with efforts to bring about a professorship for me" (1977a, 56f). According to Weinzierl, "As a Nazi from the Austrian Fascists, Wenzel Count Gleispach had been compulsorily retired with pension. As Rector of the University of Vienna in the academic year 1929–1930 he promulgated a new student order which foresaw the education of student nations." After the use of strike troops against Jewish and socialist students, this new order was declared illegal and cancelled (Weinzierl 1981, 81). He took part "as the only Rector, in the 13th student-day in Breslau in July 1930, which by then was strongly influenced by the National-Socialist 'Body of German Students' [*Studentenschaft*]" (Ibid., 78).

20. Kurt Schilling (1899–1977), a private instructor, was from 1937 professor in Munich, and from 1933 member of the NS-Party (See Henckmann 1987, 23 ff.). He was commissioned by the SS-Ancestral Heritage Project to construct a "Philosophy Section," but establishing it never came about (see Simon among others; on the relation of Schilling to Heidegger, see Woehl, among others).

21. Richard Harder (1896–1957), a student of Werner Jaeger, became a professor in Münster in 1923. He was editor of the journal, *Gnomon*. In 1933 he entered the SA. He criticized the terrorism of the NS-Student Group in Kiel. He was a collaborator with the Rosenberg Office, and, among other things with Alfred Baeumler on the "High School" Project (See Loseman 1977, 143f).

22. Gadamer writes, "When the Americans occupied Leipzig, I was study-

ing two newly published books, volumes 2 and 3 of Werner Jaeger's *Paideia*.— It is also an odd fact that this book by an 'emigrant,' written in German and published by a German publisher, could be published during the years of the highest need during the war. Total war?" (1977b, 76) Werner Jaeger (1888– 1961), who was married to a Jewish woman, traded his Berlin chair in classical philology for a professorship in Chicago. Minister of Sciences Rust let it be conveyed that he wanted to express to Jaeger his "simultaneous thanks for his academic activities and the approval of his profession" (cited according to Lose- man 1977, 43). Loseman also notes, "The special place of Jaeger was also heeded at a later time. According to a secret order to the press in 1941, the men- tion of Jaeger was allowed, but after "greatest hesitation and prior consultation back and forth with the ZP Department of the Cultural Press." (Ibid.)

23. Aloys Wenzl (1887–1967) was a professor in Munich beginning in 1933. According to Henkmann, "In the winter semester of 1935–1936 and in the summer semester of 1936, he was not allowed to continue lecturing because as longtime member of the SPD (1918–1933) and during his tenure as lecturer he had been attacked as a Marxist in disguise and as an insidious pacifist. In 1938, on account of his political and philosophical thinking, his right to lecture was officially withdrawn, also because he had occupied himself, they claimed, with a 'Judaized physics' (1987, 23). Paul Tillich, who became professor in 1929 in Frankfurt as follower of Max Scheler and as spokesman for the "religious so- cialists," also lost his permission to teach and emigrated to the USA.

24. Theodor Litt (1880–1962) was from 1920 a professor in Leipzig. He was co-editor from 1925–1937 of the magazine, *Die Erziehung* (Education), and in 1937 retired at his own request. In 1941 he was forbidden to lecture. At a conference on "Education in the National-Socialist State" held at the Pedagog- ical-Psychological Institute in Munich on August 1–5, 1933, he was scheduled to give a major address on principles, but he was prevented by the National So- cialist Union of Saxony and in Litt's place Rothacker spoke. The lecture was published in 1933 under the title, *Die Stellung der Geisteswissenschaften im na- tionalsozialistischen Staate* [The Place of the Humanities/Social Sciences in the National Socialist State] (see Griederich 1989, Weber 1989a).

25. Joachim Ritter (1903–1974), a student and assistant of Ernst Cassirer (see note 4 above), was in 1932 a private instructor in Hamburg. He signed the 1933 Declaration by Professors of Support . . . for Adolf Hitler and the Na- tional-Socialist State (see note 15 above) and was active in the "NS-Welfare of the People," the "NS-Aid for the Student Struggle," and "NS-Teachers Union." In 1937 he became a member of the National Socialist Party, in 1939 he was "Political Leader" of the Rissen local group, and was active in the 1943 Call upon Kiel University. He was from 1947–1969 a professor in Münster, and

also editor of the *Historischen Wörterbuchs der Philosophie*. (See T. Cassirer 1981, Meran 1990, Weber 1989b)

26. Ferdinand Weinhandl (1896–1973) gave the "Fire Address"for the book-burning in Kiel. In 1935 he became a professor at Kiel to succeed Richard Kroner (see note 3). In 1937 he became Leader of the *Wissenschaftliche Akademie des N-S Dozentenbundes* [Academy of Sciences of the National-Socialist Teachers Union]. In 1940 he was a leader of the Philosophy Work-Group for the "Insertion of the Humanities into the War." In 1942 he became a professor in Frankfurt, and after 1944 was at Graz University. In 1966 he received the Austrian Cross of Honor First Class in Science and Art (see Leske 1990, 289).

27. Johannes Popitz (1884–1945) was Prussian Minister of Finance from 1933–1944. After the 20 July 1944 assassination attempt on Hitler, he was executed.

INDEX

167

Yale Studies in Hermeneutics
Joel Weinsheimer, Editor

Yale Studies in Hermeneutics provides a venue for inquiry into
the theory of interpretation in all its varieties and domains.
Titles in the series seek to expand and deepen our
understanding of understanding while explicitly framing and
situating themselves within the tradition of recognized
hermeneutical thinkers from antiquity to the present.

• • •

Other volumes available from Yale University Press

Gadamer's Hermeneutics
A Reading of Truth and Method
JOEL C. WEINSHEIMER

Philosophical Hermeneutics and Literary Theory
JOEL C. WEINSHEIMER

Hermeneutics Ancient and Modern
GERALD L. BRUNS

Eighteenth-Century Hermeneutics
Philosophy of Interpretation in England from Locke to Burke
JOEL C. WEINSHEIMER

Introduction to Philosophical Hermeneutics
JEAN GRONDIN
Translated by Joel C. Weinsheimer,
with a Foreword by Hans-Georg Gadamer

Hermeneutics and the Rhetorical Tradition
Chapters in the Ancient Legacy and Its Humanist Reception
KATHY EDEN

Giordano Bruno and the Kabbalah
Prophets, Magicians, and Rabbis
KAREN SILVIA DE LEÓN-JONES

Rhetoric and Hermeneutics in Our Time
A Reader
EDITED BY WALTER JOST AND MICHAEL J. HYDE

Praise of Theory
Speeches and Essays
HANS-GEORG GADAMER
Translated by Chris Dawson

Hermeneutics, Religion, & Ethics
HANS-GEORG GADAMER
Translated by Joel Weinsheimer